DUNSTABLE SCHOOL

1888-1971

Expanded from
A Short History of Dunstable School
1888-1963
by
F.M.Bancroft

The Book Castle

First published May, 2002
by
The Book Castle
12 Church Street
Dunstable
Bedfordshire LU5 4RU

Based on the booklet, published June 1963,
'A Short History of Dunstable School, 1888-1963'
by F.M.Bancroft

With additional material from the booklet, published 1988,
'Ashton Centenary, 1888- 1988'
compiled by Mrs P.M.Cleave of Manshead Upper School

Plus photographs and updates provided by members
of Dunstable School Old Boys' Association, 2002

Plus an extract from 'Bourne and Bred,' published June 1990,
© Colin Bourne

This arrangement © The Book Castle,2002

ISBN 1 903747 29 5
Scanning and layout by Monographics, Houghton Regis, Beds.
Printed by Pear Tree Press, Stevenage, Herts.

Back cover quote from 'Bourne and Bred.'

Contents

Each chapter commences with the text from F. M. Bancroft's booklet, followed by material from the other sources.

Aerial Photograph of School, 1957.

PREFACE

This brief history of Dunstable Grammar School has been written by Mr. F. M. Bancroft to commemorate the seventy fifth year of its existence. Based on School records and old magazines, the recollections of former headmasters and past and present members of staff, the memories of Old Dunstablians and friends of the school over several generations, it will I am sure, give much pleasure to all who read it, and evoke nostalgic memories for all who have been at some time or other associated with the events it describes.

The author, who has himself played a significant part for close on thirty years in the history he has written, puts us all in his debt by reminding us of the constant role that the School has played since its foundation. For while it is true that its outward appearances may be altered and the emphasis shift with the varying personalities of those entrusted with its direction; and schools are not immune from the winds of change, and must constantly adapt themselves to the shifting needs of the society which they reflect and which they serve; nevertheless the challenging and ineluctable responsibility remains—to prepare our pupils to fit happily and purposefully into the adult world around them, and to leave it, we hope, just a little better than they find it.

L. P. Banfield, 1963

E. E. Apthorp
1900 - 1915, 1918 - 1929
Second Master

W. F. BROWN
1894 - 1924
Second Master

L. C. R. Thring
Headmaster 1888 - 1921

A. R. Thompson
Headmaster 1921 - 1927

A. F. R. Evans
Headmaster 1927 - 1948

G. M. Bailey
Headmaster 1948 - 1960

L. P. Banfield
Headmaster 1960 - 1971

ARCHITECT'S DRAWING OF THE SCHOOL, 1887

Chapter One

Our Founders & Benefactors

Inside the porch at the main entrance of the school a plaque set in the wall records that Thomson Hankey Esq., Chairman of the Governors of Frances Ashton's Foundation, here laid the foundation stone on June 24th 1887. Beneath the stone were placed several gold coins and a copy of the current Dunstable Gazette. The Dunstable Borough Band was in attendance, a considerable crowd sang the hymn ''All people that on Earth do dwell'', and the local children had a holiday from school. It was a day of educational significance in the history of South Bedfordshire.

That it was possible at all was due to the charitable bequests of Mrs. Frances Ashton, who died in 1727. By her will dated March 30th of that year she appointed five trustees, who, upon her death, became her executors. Frances Ashton was the daughter of a wealthy London merchant, Thomas Chew, a name very familiar to natives of Dunstable. She bequeathed money for many charitable purposes, such as the relief of poor clergymen 'of sober life and conversation', the maintenance of six almswomen who 'attend the worship of God in the Church of England on the Sabbath Day at Dunstable', and to provide them with a 'gown and petticoat all of the same colour', the provision of bread 'to be by the Minister and Church Wardens of the Parish of Dunstable, weekly, every Sunday after morning service, distributed to the poor', and the aid of discharged prisoners. The only references in her will to money for educational purposes are 'a sum of four pounds yearly to the Charity School of St. Giles, Cripplegate', and 'thirty shillings a year or more for repairing and cleaning a clock which she had given or set, upon the School House at Dunstable'. Her will also records that her only daughter, Elizabeth, the reputed wife of John Rayner, had by her undutifulness and marriage without her consent disobliged her, and consequently was, under certain circumstances, disinherited. In fact Elizabeth Rayner died without issue, no new circumstances were created, and the original provisions of the will were carried out.

Much of Frances Ashton's estate was composed of land and farms, so that, naturally enough, its value increased considerably and to such an extent that in July 1848 the High Court approved a new scheme for the administration of the estate, whereby two separate charities were formed, one to administer the fund for the benefit of poor clergy and the other the Ashton Almshouse Charity. Money continued to accumulate and further schemes were approved by the High Court in 1884 and 1886 under which the charity became known as the 'Ashton Schools and Almshouses Foundation'.

By 1861 it had been found possible to establish the Ashton Elementary Schools near the Priory Church. The sale of property in Luton had provided for the maintenance of the Almshouses and left a balance which, by a judgement of the Court of Chancery, was applied to educational purposes. In 1868 a further sale of property to the Midland Railway Company provided the trustees with a capital sum of £14,500, This very substantial sum was surplus to the anticipated needs of the charity, and it was felt that it should be applied to some one 'special object'. Very strong views were expressed in Dunstable and the neighbourhood "that this sum of £14,500 should be appropriated to the Foundation of a Grammar School for the Education of the Sons of Professional men, tradesmen and others (in fact the Middle Classes) at a moderate expense. No such school exists nearer than Bedford and we are assured and believe it would be a great Boon to the Towns of Dunstable, Luton, and Leighton Buzzard, together with the large adjacent Villages containing a population of 40,000 souls. And we think that if £4,500 could be appropriated for the School Buildings and Masters' Houses, and £10,000 for the endowment, such a school might be founded and efficiently maintained, but we fear any much smaller sum would be inadequate". In 1871 a deputation from the Corporation of Dunstable presented a Memorial to the Trustees along the same lines. The Trustees were, in fact, not unwilling to act in accordance with the Corporation's wishes, but their hands were legally tied by the Endowed Schools Act. The Endowed Schools Commissioners were, however, succeeded by the Charity Commissioners and the Trustees were able at the beginning of 1875 to tell the Corporation that they were in communication with the Commissioners with a view to using the surplus funds for the establishment of a Grammar School. A draft scheme submitted by the Trustees was rejected, but in 1877 a public local enquiry presided over by Mr. D. R. Fearon, an Assistant Commissioner, was held at the Town Hall, Dunstable, in consequence of which Mr. Fearon represented to the Trustees that if they chose to consider the charity as a Mixed Educational Charity, under Section 24 of the Act (32 and 33 Vic. Cap 56) there would be an overwhelming proportion of the funds available for educational purposes. There were still problems to be solved concerning the administration of the charities, but eventually a suitable formula was agreed, and in 1885 received Her Majesty's signature at a meeting of the Privy Council, held at Osborne House. Certain sums were allocated for the continuance of the Almshouse Charity, provision was made for the Elementary Schools, and, subject to the approval of the Charity Commissioners a Grammar School suitable for one hundred pupils and a Headmaster's house to include room for twenty boarders was to be built as soon as possible.

Of the Trustees who began this somewhat protracted affair, only Thomson Hankey survived to welcome the new school. He, with Mrs. Ashton, may truly be called one of our early benefactors, and he it was who laid the foundation stone in 1887. His name is perpetuated by his gift of a sum of money to provide the annual

2

Hankey Gold Medal. The original Governing Board consisted of eight members, all Co-optative Governors, but it was provided that the first three of these who died or resigned should be succeeded by Representative Governors appointed by the Corporation of Dunstable. These, then, were the first Governors:

Thomson Hankey of 59 Portland Place in the county of Middlesex, Esquire .

Reginald Hankey, of 78 Ebury St. in the same county, Esquire.

The Right Hon. Arthur Wellesley Peel, of the Lodge, Sandy,
       in the County of Bedford, M.P., Speaker of the House of Commons.

The Hon. Arthur John Edward Russell, of 2 Audley Square,
       in the county of Middlesex, M.P.

Hugh Colin Smith, of 71 Prince's Gate in the same county, Esquire.

Benjamin Bennett, of Cheverells Park, near Dunstable, Esquire.

The Rev. Augustus Frederick Birch, Rector of Berkhamstead St.
    Mary, otherwise Northchurch, in the county of Hertford, Clerk

The Rev. John Heyrick Macaulay, Rector of Dunstable, Honorary Canon of Ely.

Further alterations were made to the scheme in 1903 and 1911, which separated the Schools from the Almshouses. On 3rd September 1947 an ''Instrument of Government'' was sealed appointing a new Board of Governors for "Ashton Grammar School, Dunstable" and on February 11th, 1958 there was an additional scheme creating "The Ashton Schools Foundation" which administers the income from the bequests of Frances Ashton's will as far as the Schools (the Grammar School and the Ashton Church of England Primary School, Church Street, Dunstable) are concerned.

It is interesting to note, however, through all these various schemes, there has been one constant factor. The number of Foundation or Co-optative Governors has always been five, who are the symbolic successor, to the original five trustees of Frances Ashton's will. The Grammar School Governors consist of six Foundation Governors (five being the successors to the original five with the addition of one appointed by the Committee of the Old Dunstablians' Club) and twelve representative Governors appointed by the Local Education Authority (the Beds. County Council) of whom three are nominated by the Dunstable Borough Council and one each by the Luton Borough Council, Luton Rural District Council and Leighton Buzzard Urban District Council. A representative governor need not be a member of the appointing or nominating body, There is an important qualification for a Foundation Governor on the Board of Grammar School Governors. Such a person must be a member of the Church of England, and although this has on occasions mitigated against the appointment of many otherwise eminently suitable persons, it does help to preserve the close association which has always existed between the School and the Priory Church. Vacancies among the five Foundation Governors are still filled in exactly the same way as directed by Frances Ashton in her will, by resolution of the remaining Foundation Governors.

The Ashton Schools Foundation is administered by a different Board of Governors. In this instance there are only ten governors, consisting again of the representatives of the original five trustees, known as Co-optative Governors, one of whom is, ex officio, the Rector of Dunstable and five representative governors; the Dunstable Borough Council and Bedford County Council each appointing two and the St. Alban's Diocesan Education Committee appointing the fifth.

Frances Ashton was most anxious that her executors should be encouraged to perform their duties assiduously and in comfort. She ordered that they could employ a secretary or receiver to collect rents and other revenue. The present Board still appoints a secretary but only pays him exactly the same annual salary as Frances Ashton stated should be paid to the first secretary in 1727. She also directed that the trustees should be reimbursed to the extent of £15 a year for any expenses they incurred and she bequeathed one pound annually to provide them with a dinner. Unfortunately, the present board does not enjoy either of these privileges.

Frances Ashton decreed that her trustees should meet twice a year in June and December and it is interesting to note that the present Board of the Ashton Schools Foundation also meet twice a year in the same months. Since the appointment of the new board in 1958, the income of the Foundation has again started to increase and funds will shortly become available to enable the Governors to implement other objects contained in the 1958 scheme, to the ultimate benefit of both the Schools and the pupils educated in them.

The first Clerk to the Trustees of whom we have a record is Mr. Isaac William Sewell, who took part in the negotiations to found the School. His successor was his partner, Mr. George Halliley Edwards, who was succeeded in 1911 by Mr. Leonard Nevill. Mr. Eric Nevill succeeded his father in 1937, and continued to hold the appointment until 1958, when he was succeeded by the present Clerk, Mr. A. H. Simpson, who has had a close association with the School and the Foundation since 1920.

Since the School has come under the jurisdiction of the Bedfordshire Education Committee and the Governors and the Ashton Schools Trustees have had a separate identity, the Clerk to the Governors has been the Director of Education, Mr. T. S. Lucking.

Chapter Two

The Age of Thring

September 1963 makes the 75th anniversary of the School's opening for business. A Headmaster, L. C. R. Thring, formerly an Assistant Master at Wellingborough Grammar School, had already been appointed, and Mr. & Mrs. Thring had spent much of the summer interviewing prospective pupils and parents and showing them around the new premises. They were to do this for the next thirty years. There are still many Old Boys who were at school in this time, and in all my conversations with them I have never heard an unkind word of either. Their life was devoted to the school, they regarded every boy as an additional son in a rapidly growing family, and the impression of the school as a family emerges clearly from all the magazines and documents of those days.

Fortunately one of those boys interviewed in 1888 is still alive, in the person of C. H. Dixon, who has recorded for us his early memories. "In the middle of the first week in September the school was opened for pupils, and I so well remember standing with a number of boys at the door in the playground waiting for the moment when it should open and our new school life begin. From Dunstable I remember three names very well, Oliver, Hugh Anderson and Daniels, and from Luton Ernest and Frank Gladwell, Walter Keeling and Frank Oliver. We found ourselves very soon living and working under a system none of us had experienced before, the real Public School system of strict discipline, hard work, compulsory games, and the punishment to fit the crime". For the first term there were three boarders and forty-six day boys, but term by term the numbers increased. The earlier buildings consisted of the present main building with asphalted playground, and behind it a large W.C. building, "which would not by any means stand up to the present day standards of Hygiene". The strip of grass which is now disappearing as the new laboratory block is constructed was used as a playing field until the present field was acquired in 1889. To improve the surface and level the cricket table, Mr. Thring employed squads of boys, eight to a team, to man a heavy roller. It was a popular form of punishment, and C. H. Dixon recalls, "I fancy that quite a lot of the excellence of that table surface today is due to the time I spent on the roller". The main building itself consisted of the Headmaster's house, the boys' dining room, a changing room, two class rooms (one of which became used as a library), a Masters' Common Room (which continued to be so used until converted some fifteen years ago into the Secretary's office), and the Hall which was used for general purposes, and where several forms were taught simultaneously if not always harmoniously.

Records of these early times are, unfortunately, far from complete, and of the earliest members of the staff little is known. J. Healing, who lived in Dunstable till

5

comparatively recently, assisted his brother-in-law when the school opened; there was also a Mr. Clarke who taught Mathematics, and a French master whose name has not survived. In 1890 J. T. Phillipson became second master (the term is now Deputy Head), and stayed until 1894. He maintained a very close connection with the School and took an active part later in the Old Boys' Association when he was Headmaster of Christ's College, Finchley. The link established, between the two schools still remains. In 1894 he was succeeded by W. F. Brown, and in 1900 E. E. Apthorp was appointed to the staff, straight from his Golf successes at Cambridge, where he gained his Blue. Thring, Brown, Apthorp, these are names which dominate the first thirty years of the school's life. Neither Brown nor Apthorp married, they lived at the school and the school was their life. In those days academic success, though valuable and often achieved, was not as important for the boy starting out in life as it is today. Examination pressures were less, and the school was expected to turn out young men of character and general all round ability rather than specialists in some particular sphere of knowledge. The personal influence of Thring, Brown and Apthorp can never be over estimated; they were directly in the tradition of Dr. Arnold. Each gave a lifetime of service.

During the first ten years many of the later features of the school began. The first Hankey Gold Medal was won in 1890 by W. Gray, whose brother, Amos, was later to serve as a School Governor, as "the best all round boy in the school". A library was opened and in 1896 a magazine (priced 6d.) appeared for the first time. It lost money. There was already a Dramatic Society, an Old Boys' Association was formed, and by the turn of the century annual dinners were being held at the Holborn Restaurant. The first secretary to the Old Boys' Association was Oliver Anderson. A Swimming Bath had already been constructed, and in 1900 came the first of the Cricket Weeks, which were to be repeated for the next thirty years. Sport played an enormous part in school life, soccer and cricket being the main games. The present Headmaster has referred to 'those halcyon days when Mr. Thring could advertise for a leg-break howler willing to teach a little Mathematics or English", and if in fact this is an exaggeration it is true in essence. Hockey came in 1902 to occupy the first part of the Spring term, the second half being devoted to Athletics, which were not allowed to interfere with the cricket. Apart from the School matches there were Club matches in which both masters and boys played, and also Staff matches for masters and their friends or visitors to the school. A fine summer afternoon was often an excuse for a half-day's holiday; during a prolonged period of winter frost opportunities were readily found for an afternoon's skating.

This must have been a fairly general picture of life at such a school as ours at such a time. The peace of the Victorian eventide was disturbed but not shattered by the South African War. The theatre of war was sufficiently remote not to interfere with everyday life, but there was a very real concern for the young men who volunteered to serve on the veldt. Among them were a number of the Dunstablians, of whom two gave their lives, the brothers H. & J. Anderson.

In 1902, F. S. Kelly, a friend of the school, gave a Pianoforte Recital, from the profits of which the Fives Courts were built. He survived to die in action in the 1914-18 war, after having won the D.S.O. By 1902 the school numbers reached 119, the highest figure so far. F. H. Webb was at school in those days. He recalls that the upper storey of the main building was used as dormitories and that the Science Laboratory was sited in the basement below the VIth form room. A number of boys travelled by train from Luton, each carriage having a carriage Prefect who was responsible for keeping order. At one time Sgt. Major Holt, also a Beefeater, at the Tower, travelled by the morning train for this purpose, It was customary for the Senior Prefect travelling to fall-in the party and march them to school. Later this duty was discharged by the famous Sgt. Major Odell who remained at the school with an interval for war service, till 1936. He first joined the School staff in 1903. In appearance a typical Sgt. Major who might well have directed drill on the school field while he himself remained in the High Street, he was the kindliest and most courteous of men, and his memory remains fragrant to this day. Another memory of F. H. Webb is the occasion when A. O. Jones, later to captain England, played in the Old Boys' Cricket Week. His brother was a local doctor, and A. O. Jones' grave is to be found in Dunstable cemetery. During the first quarter of the century Bedfordshire played a number of County matches on the School field. In 1905 A. F. Morcom gained his Cricket Blue at Cambridge, and afterwards represented the Gentlemen against the Players.

Cricket XI 1901.

A few years later C. B. Ponsonby who afterwards captained Worcestershire was at school, and with the Head and Mr. Apthorp playing for Bedfordshire the school cricket tradition was well maintained, though even in those days there were criticisms in the Magazine of the non-attendance of day boys at school matches. The Magazine itself was frequently in difficulties, and at one time the experiment was introduced of importing stories of school life or potted biographies from some agency. Fortunately the experiment was short lived.

Part of the teaching of English in those days consisted of the reading aloud of the Classics. J. A. Webdale recalls Mr. Thring's favourite as "The Idylls of the King," and W. F. Brown reading from "Pickwick Papers". Mr. Brown used to teach in the room above the Science Laboratories, and frequently complained of the smell of the products there. He recalls, too, the building of the present Laboratories, a great event of the time. Dog Kennel path, which originally went along the Head's garden and down the avenue of Chestnut trees to the boundary of Messrs. Waterlow's, had to be diverted in order to accommodate the new building. When W. D. Coales joined the staff in 1909 he was told that a further laboratory building would be built within three or four years. He retired in 1959, still awaiting it. Other features of those years were the introduction of a House System, the revival of Hockey in 1911, the beginning of the school steeplechase held on Cook's farm, and later continued through the kindness of Mr. & Mrs. Gurney, and the establishment of chocolate and blue as the school colours. The Eton jacket, the wide stiff collar and the straw boaters were features of the school dress and continued to be so in greater or less degree until 1939 when less formal clothing became necessary. Speech Day was normally held at the end of the Summer term, the great event of the academic year being the periodical examination by the London School of Examiners, in the course of which every boy in the school submitted written papers and was afterwards orally examined in every subject. How long all this took has not been recorded, but at least the Examiners must have been fairly busy people. Speeches were followed by the Past & Present Cricket Match. A feature of the occasion was the singing of the School Song; perhaps one day its sentiment may be replaced by something more acceptable to newer generations.

****

SPEECH DAY - 1899

based on a report by the London School of Examiners

"Speech Day" this year fell on Saturday, July 29th, on which occasion there was again a large gathering of the boys' parents and friends in the School Hall. The Governors were represented by Mr. Hugh Smith (Chairman), Mr. R. M. Harvey, the Rev. Canon Macaulay, Mr. George W. E. Russell, Mr. B. Bennett,

Mr. H. Hankey, and Mr. G. H. Edwards. The Rev. Paul Wyatt, of Bedford, distributed the prizes, and among those present were Sir Edgar Sebright, the Mayor of Dunstable (Alderman F. T. Garrett), Major C. S. Benning, and many others.

The detailed report of the examination having been read, in which particular praise was given to the excellence of Hare's Classics and Watkin's Mathematics, Mr. Reynolds Squire, M.A., F.R.S.L., who made a viva voce examination of the School, in summing up, said that the general results were highly satisfactory. The classical knowledge shown by the boys of the Upper VI Form deserved the highest praise, and would rank with that expected at any of our best, especially classical, schools. Hare's Greek was also entirely satisfactory, and his name should be heard of in the near future as an honour to the School.

The Lower VI was a very fair Form, but there was a great difference between individual members. He found on the whole, the grammar had improved since last year. The examination of Form V in French was most satisfactory, Hansard being especially good all round, while Martin shone in conversation. Holloway, Hyder, and Lenthall might also be mentioned. In Latin, the syntax was a little deficient, but the work was uniformly very fair.

Form III was an intelligent class, Wilson and Rosson ii. being good in French, and Wilson's Latin, as well as that of Bayly and Shaw, being well done.

The writing of Form II was bold, clear and good, but the spelling was uncertain. All the boys came in to do their best, and did it. Mr. Squire summed up his report as follows:- A day spent in reviewing the boys gave an outsider a fair estimate of the tone prevailing throughout the School. This tone, he said without reserve, was good. The boys were cheery, well mannered, obedient, and thoroughly nice fellows. The work had evidently been done thoroughly and conscientiously both by teachers and learners.

In conclusion, he said the Council was of opinion, from the above report, that the School was in a highly satisfactory condition. They would especially draw atten tion to the fact that, in addition to providing a sound general education, the School had shown itself able to produce very promising candidates both in Classics and Mathematics.

It might be anticipated that the School list of University distinctions will receive additions at no distant date. The report of their examiners in Chemistry was: They would therefore tender to the Head Master and his staff their congratulations on the nature of the report, and their thanks for the facilities afforded them during the examination.

****

THEY DIED FOR THEIR COUNTRY

(from the July 1901 school magazine)
A report concerning the Deaths in the Boer War of
H & J Anderson

When the call came for men, and that unparalleled outburst of enthusiastic patriotism swept through the country, the little town of Dunstable was in no way behind with offers of loyal sons. For the first time in history, members of our Volunteer Forces were invited to enlist for active service, and in the first Active Service Company of volunteers sent out to our Bedfordshire Regiment in South Africa, Dunstable had four lads; others had offered, but for various reasons had not been accepted. Of those four selected, the Dunstable School had the proud distinction of claiming two as former scholars - Privates Hugh and John Anderson.

Let it be recorded, that on the first occasion when England required assistance from her soldier-citizen sons, the Dunstable School gave two of its former scholars. Private Hugh Anderson died at Sanna's Post, O.R.C., of dysentery, on February 24th. Writing of him, his Commanding Officer said : "He was the life and soul of the company, when on the trek or on short rations; always ready to look on the bright side of things. He was a good soldier and did his duty well. We shall miss him in many ways."

Of Private John Anderson, Captain Fox, writing home to a friend, said:- "I have just met one of Mr. Anderson's sons (near Thaba N'chu). The boy has made a fine soldier." That was some months before his death, when Private John Anderson was also full of buoyant life and courage, albeit he was eagerly looking forward to the home-coming that had, even then, been promised our Bedfordshire Volunteers. But for him, as for his brother, there was to be no earthly home-coming.

Hearing that his brother was dangerously ill, he rode in to Thaba N'chu on February 21st to see him, but arrived too late; five hours before he reached that place Hugh had been sent back on the way to the Bloemfontein hospital. He died half-way on the journey, and four days later Private John Anderson received the sad news of his death. On the previous day John had also to report sick with dysentery. He lay in a tent hospital at Thaba N'chu for a week, and was then removed to a house. On March 9th he wrote home: "Twelve months today we landed in S. Africa. Our year's service is now completed, and I hope it will not be long before we sail for home."

By a pathetically sad coincidence, the news of his death had reached Dunstable through the medium of the War Office casualty list the day before the arrival of that letter. He had recovered from dysentery, had rejoined his Company on out post duty west of Thaba N'chu, but had fallen a victim there to enteric. He died at Bloemfontein on March 31st.

During his period of active service in S. Africa he acted as correspondent for the Dunstable Borough Gazette and a series of seventeen articles he wrote entitled "With our Volunteers in South Africa", gave a picturesque and interesting history of their movements and the life they led in the campaign, which reflected considerable credit on his School training. Our hearts ache for the loss of these lads, but we have the grand, consoling thought that, bravely and willingly, they offered themselves in the hour of England's necessity; bravely, too, they died for their country.

A W Mooring

****

Chapter Three

The End of an Age

The school was now more than twenty years old. Its very success was to create new problems. L. C. R. Thring owed something to his connection with the famous Thring of Uppingham and to a family association with the educational firm of Gabbitas & Thring, but his own personal qualities and the motherly influence of Mrs. Thring were vital in building up the family. L. A. Boskett, then a boy at school and for many years after a member of staff, remembers the affection in which they were universally held. Many boys boarded at Dunstable whose parents were overseas in the service of the Crown, and many foreign boys were educated here. At one period there were boys from France, Italy, America, China and India. Of these we heard only recently of T. W. C. Chun, still working as an architect and civil engineer in Hong Kong. K. W. Nazimuddin played a great part in the creation of Pakistan and served for a time as its Prime Minister. He visited the school while in England for a Prime Minister's conference. Gary Cooper and his brother, natives of Dunstable, returned from America to attend school here. The connection between Dunstable and J. T. Phillipson, Head of Christ' s College, Finchley must have influenced may Finchleians to send their sons here when a well known Finchley school closed, just as later the closing of Elstow School led to a number of its pupils transferring to Dunstable. What with extensions to the buildings and increasing costs of administration to be paid, the funds of the original endowment proved to be inadequate, and from 1911 onwards the Bedfordshire County Council agreed to support the school by making up the deficit at the end of each year, an arrangement which was to continue for the remainder of Mr. Thring's time.

In 1914 came the Great War, the impact of which was felt no less in Dunstable than elsewhere. Numbers of the Old Boys rushed to enlist for service in the war which was to be over by Christmas. Some military authorities of those days were prone to judge the success of an operation by the number of casualties sustained; they would have rated Dunstable's contribution highly, as from this comparatively small school sixty-two gave their lives. Many won considerable distinction, notably Col. E. E. D. Henderson, who won the Victoria Cross near Kut-el-Amara, in January 1917. Mr. & Mrs. Thring were deeply affected by the loss of so many of their boys, and the crowning blow came when they heard of the death in action of 'Teddy' Thring, their only son. Yet the numbers in the school continued to increase; with 67 boarders and 100 day boys in 1917, accommodation was severely taxed, and the staff records of those days show plainly how difficult it was to obtain suitable men to teach. The able bodied left for military service; only the medically unfit and those invalided out remained. It was not until 1919 or 1920 that a more settled and adequate teaching staff could be restored. This, of course, was common enough, other schools were in the same position, but the strain of these years was taking an increasing toll of Mr. & Mrs. Thring, and in the early part of 1921 Mr. Thring announced that he proposed to retire at the end of the Summer term.

The Thring family possessed its own coat of arms, the family motto was "Do the right and fear not".

It was on this basis that Mr. & Mrs. Thring founded their lives here — passing to well-earned retirement in Somerset they left behind ties of affectionate remembrance which have lasted beyond their death. L. C. R. Thring died some twelve years later. Mrs. Thring survived until 1949. Materially they left a school far different from the infant of 1888. From the start of 3 boarders and 46 day boys the numbers had increased to 82 boarders and 179 day boys. The School house had been completed; Ashton Lodge had been built to house 3 masters and 21 boarders. The original staff of 1 Assistant Master had grown into a staff of 11 resident masters and 4 non-resident masters.

Whole school photograph, approx 1919.

L. C. R. THRING

(from a 1911 school magazine)

"In our Head we have a man who, with his sterling qualities and splendid character, has always set a noble example and appealed to the best instincts of his boys. He has from the first earned their respect and something far greater, that is, their affection... he is stern enough when occasion desires, as all disciplinarians must be, but to judge him properly, you must see him in school, and then out of school joining in the outdoor sports and excelling at them all in a way that wins the admiration of those privileged to be present."

The same writer speaks of Mrs. Thring as "a kind and gracious lady". She it was who, with the help of a School Matron, had the job of looking after the gradually increasing numbers of boarders, some of whom, as the years passed, came from as far afield as France, Italy, America, China and India. Her husband was a very able and enthusiastic cricketer and another magazine article recalls that "Our heartiest congratulations go to the Head on scoring a brilliant century against Felstead for the MCC."

****

THE FIRST WORLD WAR

Two things seem to emerge from a study of the school magazines of this period. Neither of them is very surprising, but each of them seems to add to a definite impression of the School as it then was. Firstly, there were the very close links which "the many Old Dunstablians who have nobly responded to the call of Duty" (as Mr. Thring wrote) maintained with their old school, and secondly the way that the everyday concerns of the school seemed to continue in these difficult and often heartbreaking circumstances.

1914 was recorded as not a good year for football, because of the lack of strong forwards. Four pounds was collected towards the Prince of Wales Fund for the Belgian refugees, though it was felt that some boys could have given more generously. The annual play that year was 'Aladdin and Out!' duly performed at the Town Hall, with Mr. Coales, a popular Science Master and swimming coach, as the Emperor. All proceeds were sent to the Red Cross Fund.

In the following year, the Summer 1915 magazine commented happily that "few have been hunted out of the library" for bad behaviour, and that no books had been lost. This was the year in which Nelson Elgood, an Old Dunstablian, wrote to his former Headmaster, from the Front, "We are still as busy as ever, with lots of work to keep us amused". Such work included supervising his Company in digging a communication trench, laying a new fire trench, and working on the construction of a footbridge. N. Elgood was later to be awarded the Military Cross, and in 1920 became Assistant Professor of Engineering at St Andrew's University. Elgood's letter was one of many which found their way to Dunstable. One father, whose son, W. H. Brantom of the Civil Service Rifles, had earlier won the DCM, wrote to Mr. Thring of his son's death in action:

"He has done credit to the tuition received at Dunstable School".

1916 was the year of a severe mumps epidemic which had quite an effect on the sports fixtures of the time. The weather was cold and wet, and there was no official Speech Day. It was a popular year for swimming - apparently, during the dinner hour, many boys were to be found "splashing and fooling about in the Baths" and there were a record number of boys who learned to swim. There was a brief lived "photographic mania". Also in 1916 some boys began to cultivate their own small vegetable gardens. They grew lettuces, peas, beans and potatoes, towards the War effort. Mr. Thring himself converted part of the playing fields into a potato patch'. Many boys and some staff, including the Head, gave up part of their summer holiday to help the local farmers in their fields, because of the shortage of labourers. In the Christmas 1916 magazine, the Headmaster records that:
"A large number of Old Boys took an active part in the Big Push (the Battle of the Somme) which began on the 1st July."

As the War continued, many notices of the deaths of Old Boys began to appear in the school magazines - by the end of the War, there were more than sixty. There were also many visits from those on leave, some of whom brought their families, and red letter days were those on which the school received a visit from Sergeant Major Odell, who did not return permanently from active service until 1919. Over the war period, the Cadet Corps grew in strength and a Bugle Band was formed. Complete with "drum and fife," it made its first appearance on Speech Day, 1919. Seven guineas had been raised by subscription and the Band had acquired its own drum. The Cadet Corps now consisted of 160 members.

P. M. Cleave

Chapter Four

The Twenties

The new Headmaster was A. R. Thompson, who had previously been Senior Mathematical Master at Berkhamstead, and at Bedford Modern School. With Mrs. Thompson he had been in charge of the principal boarding house at Bedford. Mr. & Mrs. Thompson are now living in retirement in Sussex, and Mr. Thompson has been kind enough to contribute some reminiscences of Dunstable School in his day.

"The outstanding feature of the school when I first arrived there, and what was heartening to an incoming Headmaster, was the friendly, happy family atmosphere which pervaded everything. Mr. & Mrs. Thring had fostered this attitude all the years they had been there. Their last years were made difficult by the war and its aftermath, and it was owing to the co-operation of staff and boys that the effects were not more noticeable. Mr. Thring had gathered round him some outstanding personalities, among whom were W. F. Brown and E. E. Apthorp, both of whom were bachelors who lived at the school and gave their whole lives to its welfare. It was this close touch between masters and boys which created this feeling of a family. The games, especially the cricket, were used to foster this feeling.

On the other hand, the conditions inside the school were unsatisfactory, the class-rooms were too few for the numbers in the school, and the furnishing and decoration had deteriorated during the difficult war years. With the interest and help of the Governing Body under the chairmanship of Canon Baker and the local Education Authority these things were gradually righted. A library was furnished and equipped as a memorial to the Old Boys who gave their lives in the war, and a block of class rooms was built, the science block was improved".

At this time the school was placed on the Direct Grant list and financial problems were in this way rather eased. H. J. Butters, who served the school so loyally for thirty years, had already come after war service. E. A. G. Marlar, later Headmaster of Whitgift School, was a considerable acquisition, and a Preparatory Department under C. L. Harris began in Ashton Lodge. During the previous decade, Carl Heldman, son of the novelist Joseph Conrad, had been a member of the staff. Now Robert Keable, a man of brilliant literary talents, came to teach History and English, though his stay was short. C. P. le Huray, the author of a distinguished book on his native Guernsey, stayed twenty years. W. D. Coales after an absence of two years returned to take charge of School science. The war damage to the staff was gradually repaired. During the summer term of 1922 a Garden Fete raised the very considerable sum of £700, destined to be spent in the renovation of the Sports Pavilion and the Swimming Baths.

A. R. Thompson was anxious to increase the number of boys staying on in school to take Public Examinations. It is interesting to note that in 1922 there were still only 17 candidates for the Cambridge Senior Locals (corresponding to the G.C.E. 'O' levels of today). Too many boys were removed from school at the age of 15. Even the 17 candidates previously mentioned were an improvement on earlier figures. The problem of the VIth form was to remain for many years, and the development of industry in this area has meant that those boys who have taken the School Certificate examination have always had a ready market for their services, and many who could well have stayed on and made their way to the universities preferred or sometimes were obliged to leave school in view of the prospects outside. By 1923 there were 20 candidates, and three for the Higher Certificate. The Headmaster was able to announce that H. B. Franklin had won an Open Scholarship to the Royal College of Science. This was the first year that Speech Day and Founders' Day were combined, a practice continued until very recently, when the two occasions have been separated. By an overwhelming vote the School decided to replace Soccer by Rugby; the first season was very successful. The Glee Club now made its first appearance. It flourished for over twenty years first under G. W. Hedges and then under L. A. Boskett, with Miss Florence Perry as both soloist and sometime accompanist, and came to perform many delightful concert versions of the Gilbert and Sullivan operas. By 1924 the new classrooms (ever since known as the New Buildings) together with the games changing rooms were in use.

1924 was an important year. It saw the retirement of W. F. Brown, who had been Second Master for thirty years, a vital link with the school's earliest days. Of him a contemporary has said, "No boys can have attended his classes without being influenced by the depth and sincerity of his own religious feelings, his largeness of heart, and keen sense of fair play". Now the Old Boys had raised sufficient funds for the War Memorial Library. O. G. Anderson, Chairman of the Old Dunstablians' Club, handed the key to Canon Baker as Chairman of the Governors, and the unveiling of the library was performed by the Earl of Clarendon, who had had a long association with the Ashton Trust. The general progress and development of Sixth form work continued happily and the Preparatory Department was beginning to play an increasing part in school life. One of the interesting features of this department, under first C. L. Harris and afterwards J. G. Matthewman was a series of dramatic productions and historical pageants on the lawn of Ashton Lodge, which gave much pleasure both to those taking part and those who watched. While presenting the prizes at Speech Day, 1925, Mr. C. H. Greene, Headmaster of Berkhamstead School, referred to the ancient pageant of Dunstable in connection with the forthcoming second centenary of the death of Mrs. Ashton. He recalled that there was a school at Dunstable early in the eleventh century, and that the first theatrical performance in England was given by the pupils. The Headmaster was one Geoffrey, who was invited to come from France to be Headmaster at St. Albans School. He arrived late and found another master had been appointed, whereupon he started a school at Dunstable. In the year 1110 he decided to produce a miracle play, and to make this more effective he borrowed some coats from the sacristan of St. Albans Cathedral. Geoffrey was a most unfortunate man, because after the play was produced his house was burnt down and the coats were destroyed. Thereupon he gave up the school and went to St. Albans to spend the rest of his life in making coats to replace those that were lost. He afterwards became Abbot of St. Albans.

Among the school servants were several remarkable men. Tom Brown, who looked after the playing field for many years and provided some wonderful pitches, was a real character. His name figures frequently in early magazines as a Bedfordshire cricket professional. One day he died quite suddenly on the field where he had spent so much of his life. In the school house were Joy and his wife, looking after the dining hall. They were later joined by Sidgwick, nicknamed Sorrow. Joy was very melancholy, Sorrow quite the reverse. The stoker was 'Old May', who was, when the occasion demanded, stone deaf. The police called on him one day and searched his 'cubby hole' for obscene literature. They found instead a large number of books of cultural interest, and on his death he was found to have left quite a valuable library.

It was a severe blow when A. R. Thompson left in 1927 to become Headmaster of Solihull School. He bequeathed a substantial memorial in the material improvements made during his stay, the classroom block, improved tennis and fives courts, electric light for gas (gone were the days, happily recalled by certain Old Boys, when it was possible by blowing down a gas tap at the school entrance to extinguish all the lights.) But there was a development and improvement in Scholarship, just coming to fruition at the time of his departure. Above all, both he and Mrs. Thompson cared deeply for the character and welfare of every boy. They were to remain at Solihull for twenty years where this impact was to be even more noticeable.

****

EDMUND EAST APTHORP

(from a 1943 school magazine)
An Appreciation by P. G. Bond

Edmund East Apthorp, formerly Classics master at Dunstable School, whose death has just been announced, will be mourned by Old Dunstablians all over the world. He was the ideal schoolmaster. He taught for the love of the game and because he loved and understood boys. In return they loved and admired him.

His surname lent itself to the singularly apposite nick-name "Appy," and as "Appy" he was known from his very early days in Dunstable until his retirement in 1929. And "Appy" summed up that large, benign figure perfectly.

He had a ready smile and kindly word for everyone, in his dealings he was just, in his friendships loyal; and he was ever sensitive to the finer values of life. He could converse brilliantly upon a variety of subjects, and his sense of humour never failed him.

He was a great sportsman in the best sense of the word. His exploits with the cricket bat are becoming almost legendary when big hitting is mentioned in Bedfordshire conversation, but with whatever feats prosperity may credit him, it is the unvarnished fact that he hit balls right over the old mill bordering the school ground - Gargantuan shots - and it was common gossip in the lower school that "Appy" can hit a hockey ball twice as far, using one hand, as anybody else in the school can, using two. At golf, too, he was that rare phenomenon, a "plus" man, and captained Cambridge University in his year.

His study in Ashton Lodge was a treasure-house of literary adventure for a boy, and none sought in vain access to that enchanted library, where Long John Silver rubbed shoulders with Robespierre and Danton; and old Izaak Walton came near to casting his line into the romantic waters of the Hellespont. No wonder "Appy" was the most beloved and popular of masters.

In these troublous days this country can ill afford to lose or forget the example and precept of men of the calibre of Edmund Apthorp.

Of him it might truly be said:

> His life was gentle; and the elements
> So mixed in him that Nature might stand up
> And say to all the world, "This was a man!"

Perhaps one of the best pieces of appreciation of the 'Grand Triumvirate', as Thring, Brown and Apthorp were known, is the poem written in their memory by H. E. Hunt, an Old Dunstablian then resident in Australia.

> As boys preparing for the world of men
>   (Now proved a world whose evil still rides high),
> We met three mentors, greater now than then,
>   Whose influence on our lives can never die.
> Tiggy the kindly, loved as few are loved,
>   Belgy the gentle, dwelling among his books,
> Appy the strong, with interests that moved
>   From Greek to skates "sixes" and fishing hooks
> Now each is gone to whatsoever waits
>   Beyond the last bell in the world of school;
> But they have helped to mould our lives and fates,
>   And we thank God for their ungrudging rule.

Chapter Five

The Thirties

The reign of A. F. R. Evans as Headmaster began, of course, in 1927, but it was to span the thirties and the years of the second war. An ex naval officer, he came to us from Stamford School where he had been a Housemaster and Head of Mathematics. Immediately on arrival he suffered a great blow in the loss of Mrs. Evans, who suffered a severe breakdown from which she never recovered, but he did not allow this to affect his work at the school, into the life of which he threw himself wholeheartedly .

From the first his concern was to continue the efforts made by A. R. Thompson to increase the number of boys remaining at school into the VIth form and to raise the standards simultaneously. Both he and the staff felt it necessary, in view of the national conditions of the time, that our boys should have the best guidance possible on the opportunities for them in the outside world, and accordingly a Careers Advisory Committee was formed to collect and circulate information about careers and to establish contact with employers and others specially qualified to give advice and assistance to boys leaving school. The response in those days was slow and not as wholehearted as it has more recently become. There was then no Youth Employment Service, and few schools had Careers Masters. The committee operated from 1932 to 1948. The Headmaster was Chairman, L. A. Boskett, C. P. le Huray, and W. T. Lack served as staff members; H. J. Darby, A. Gray, and E. H. Woods represented the Governors, J. Hillier served on behalf of the Old Dunstablians Club, F. M. Bancroft served as Asst. Secretary while A. C. Wadsworth was Secretary. When the Dunstable Youth Employment Committee was formed A. C. Wadsworth became the Grammar Schools representative, serving as Vice-Chairman 1949-58, and Chairman 1958-62. The Committee did valuable work in helping boys to choose careers wisely and in guiding the early years of those careers. Employers came to recognise that the recommendation of the committee was in itself a worth-while qualification. P. A. W. Harrington is now Careers Master.

In 1929, E. E. Apthorp retired, the last of the great triumvirate. In 1929 also began the series of school visits abroad; the first one was to Belgium under the guidance of C. P. le Huray. and there have heen many more over the years, notably with R. L. Poirier to France, with H. J. Butters and F. Cadle to Germany and the exchange Hockey visits which were so popular in the 1930s, and in post war days with B. C. Arthur to France, and K. A. Davies and J. C. Wood for ski-ing parties. Two names which figure prominently in the magazines of those days are H. E. Hunt, a regular and valued contributor, and later a faithful correspondent from Australia where he took Holy Orders, and Dr. O Meara, a lovable eccentric, who was most generous in his gifts to young cricketers and to the School Library.

A General Inspection in 1930 revealed an all round improvement in school standards. The post 1918 years had made it clear that in so competitive a world as

After the annual Founders' Day Service at the Priory Church, 1937.

had developed while character was important, qualifications were also necessary. The 1930s saw the extension of the New Buildings by the addition of two class-rooms and extended changing facilities. There followed on the building of the new Gymnasium and Woodwork Room, necessary to house adequately the growing number of boys. Yet the proportion of juniors to seniors remained inequitable. In 1932, of 20 boys in the school only 60 were over 14 years of age, a factor which reflected adversely on the VIth form and on school teams. By 1935 the numbers had risen to 270, and they have steadily increased ever since, but it is only in very recent years that we have been able to maintain a VIth form at all fitting to the needs of the school. The year 1934 saw the death of W. F. Brown, and L. C. R. Thring. The Thring Memorial subscribed by the Old Boys was a Changing Room and Filter Plant for the School Baths. The scattered nature of the school buildings led to the introduction in 1935 of an internal telephone system, in theory a splendid scheme though in practice it has never quite realised expectations. In the early 1930s, prob-ably for economic reasons, the number of boarders declined, reaching its lowest point in 1934 when there were 9 boarders. To improve the position the Governors offered two Boarding Scholarships each year, and gradually the position improved until early in the war the Boarding House had over 40 members. As distinct from the Old Boys' dinners a number of functions were held at this time for former boarders; they were popular and well attended. Those at school in those days will remember Miss Draper, who retired in 1939. A tall straight-backed Victorian lady, who did not compromise with modern fashions, Miss Draper instilled a real love of Art into several generations of schoolboys.

In March 1937 a Parents' Association was formed under the inspiration of C. Hyder, for many years Secretary of the Old Dunstablians Club, and later to be Chairman of the Governors. The aims of the Association were to co-operate with the Headmaster and Staff by providing financial assistance for the further education of boys who might otherwise have had to leave school, to organise meetings between Parents and Staff, encourage matches between Parents and the School; and to help, without interference, in every way possible in the school's general welfare. Amos Gray was elected President, F. G. Wilkes Treasurer, R. B. T. Dinsdale Asst. Secretary and C. Hyder, Secretary, It made a promising start, but unhappily failed to survive the war years,

In 1938 the School celebrated its 50th birthday; the occasion was marked by a four day Festival. The first day was marked by a P.T. Display and a Swimming Gala, followed by a concert sponsored by the Old Dunstablians and the Parents' Association in the Speech Hall. On the second day the School combined with the Old Boys to face the M.C.C., captained by the Rev. E. T. Killick of Cambridge and England, and a glorious day's cricket ended with the M.C.C. just avoiding defeat. In the evening the Dramatic Society presented three one-act plays. The third day featured the Old Boys' match and a school tea provided by the Parents' Association. It was followed by a Cadet Corps display, and the evening was rounded off by a memorable Pierrot Concert. The Festival concluded with an address by Canon E. F. Bonhote, the Master of Haileybury, at the Priory Church on the Sunday morning. Few could have realised that these splendid and moving celebrations marked the end of another era, or that many of those who took part in them would shortly be playing their part in a much larger theatre where the rewards of success and failure were life and death.

****

R.S.M. ODELL
A memory

In 1903 one of the school's most famous 'characters' joined the school staff as a drill instructor, R.S.M. Odell, who for some time escorted the young commuters from the station to the School, as part of his duties. He remained at the school until 1936, with a break for War service. Sergeant Major Odell has been called a 'stern disciplinarian' but also "the kindliest and most courteous of men". When the Cadet Corps was founded at the school, it was in the hands of R.S.M Odell and the school's Armoury Room was his domain. Mr. Eric Baldock remembers Sergeant Odell in the 1920's when, as an enthusiastic schoolboy, he, Mr. Baldock, marched up to the school gate where Sgt. Odell was standing, and saluted him smartly.

1932: Regimental Sergeant-Major Odell poses with his smallest cadet, K.F.Jeffs.

"You must NEVER salute an NCO, boy," said the Sergeant sternly.

"Then may I salute a gentleman?" asked young Baldock.

Mr. Baldock's contemporary, Mr. Eric Snoxell, recalls being on CC manoeuvres on the school field when a sharp hailstorm blew up from Dunstable Downs. "That's where your enemy is'" the Sergeant encouraged his young recruits. The Sergeant also ran the school's first Tuck Shop, adjacent to the stairway by the school's main entrance. I should imagine that strict order was maintained.

In the cold January weather of 1941, R.S.M Edgar Odell died, at the age of seventy-two. Thirty years and more of those had been spent in the service of Dunstable School. Many remembered with gratitude the training he had given them, and some of his favourite sayings - "We're not playing at shops!" to an unsatisfactory line at Church Parade, and "Hurry along, please!" to tardy boys and masters on their way to prayers. "Old Sergeant Major" was accompanied on his last journey to Church by a guard of honour of his old regiment, the 5th Bedfordshires, with whom he had been when badly wounded at Suvla Bay in 1915, on the way to Gallipoli. The Last Post was played over his grave by Sergeant J. Jory, of the Cadet Corps.

P. M. Cleave

****

SCHOOL DAYS

An extract from
'Bourne & Bred - A Dunstable boyhood between the wars'
by Colin Bourne

From the September day in 1888 that Dunstable Grammar School opened its doors, under the headmastership of L. C. R. Thring, it became an integral part of Dunstable. It was an asset to the town and the town accepted it as such. The building was in the town, it was of the town and it brought credit to the town. The masters played their part in the civic and social affairs of the town and all its events were reported in great detail in the local Dunstable paper. A big event like Speech Day, which incorporated the Founders' Day service and Sports Day on the school playing field would take up two whole pages. Dunstable was proud of its Grammar School and rightly so.

It was not one of the leading schools of the country. It was not expected to be and it never set out to be in the same category as a major public school, even though the school song, referring to Eton and Rugby, says 'Wait awhile, we may yet have a bard of our own'. It was not one of the topmost grammar schools, although it had been classified early on as a minor public school and boys came from distant parts of the world to be boarded there. But it *was* a grammar school, a good grammar school and it gave a sound all-round education aligned with sporting activities of note. It taught courtesy, politeness and the basic truths of life. And because of the masters over the years and a lot of the boys who went there it was a character school, with a happy atmosphere.

I was fortunate again to be there when it still had that atmosphere and when the masters were characters in themselves, even though, as I understand it, the first thirty years of the twentieth century were outstanding. Certainly I am thankful that my parents, by dint of saving and foregoing things themselves, managed to send me there. I am proud to be an Old Dunstablian, I don't mind saying so, and I only wish, along with thousands of other Old Boys, that there was still a Dunstable Grammar School.

Joining the Prep. School in the Autumn of 1933 was a happy start, which was just as well, because at the end of the summer holidays here was a big school and an utterly different environment for me. I was, however, more than ready for it and I seemed to fit in without any problem. The Prep. School, although it had its two form rooms and its joint meeting room in the creeper-covered Ashton Lodge, with its own grass lawn and flower beds outside, was part of the main school and every morning we met with the rest of the school in the Speech Hall (with the names of all the boys that had won the Hankey Gold Medal each year from 1890, inscribed in gold lettering on a brown background in panels on the walls, high up, looking down on us) for morning assembly and prayers. The forty to forty-five boys that made up the Prep. School would then repair to Ashton Lodge for lessons. But the entrance and exit gates of the school were the same for the Prep. as everyone else, so was the playing field and so were the school hours. The hours, of course, embraced the full six days of the week, with lessons in the morning only on Wednesdays and Saturdays. The half days then were for school matches. In the summer and in the lighter days of term there were two lessons in the afternoon, followed by games, but in the winter, when it was dark, games were played first and the two lessons were taken from half-past three to five o'clock. Prep. existed every night of the week and over the week-end, a great deal of it.

The Speech Hall, with some of the Hankey Gold Medal plaques around the walls.

Dress of the day was a uniform grey shirt, with grey shorts, long grey socks and black shoes. The tie was a short woollen one of horizontal stripes and the coat was a dark blue blazer with the school initials on the pocket. After two years, when I had left the Prep. and was in the senior school, it was an Eton collar in the Shells and the Third form, up to the age of fourteen, and a proper matching coat and trousers. Caps had to be worn during term at all times outside the school, although in the summer term some of the boys wore boaters. I had one in the early days, but I was not all that enthusiastic about it - it got knocked off very quickly, for one reason. Ties were either school ties of chocolate and blue, the school's colours, or house ties of various hues. My house tie for instance was yellow and black stripes.

Every boy was expected to behave himself outside the school, in the town, on public transport (a considerable number of boys came to school on a bus or on the train from Luton) and elsewhere. There was to be no unseemly behaviour and this included eating from anything or drinking a bottle of pop. The right dress and behaviour was strictly upheld and the prefects saw to that as well as any master. I thought I was perfectly safe, one late Saturday afternoon standing at the bottom of Beech Hill in Luton waiting for a bus, when I was in the Fourth, eating two penny-worth of chips. Not so. Called up to the Prefects' Study on the Monday morning, at break-time, there followed 100 lines on the avoidance of devouring chips on the public highway- "in your best handwriting, please". Dropping litter was almost as punishable an offence as being late for school or not doing your prep. Actually we never really thought of dropping anything on the pavement or elsewhere - it just wasn't done. Would I could dish out 100 lines now to all the schoolchildren (and others) who drop paper bags, cartons, cans, without a second thought on the pavement and in the road where I live now!

The master in charge of the Prep. was Mr. C. L. Harris, a man totally dedicated to the school and to the boys for whom he was responsible. He also served as a housemaster of Thompson House, one of the four houses of the main school that were named after famous masters of earlier years (Apthorp, Brown, Thompson and Thring). C. L. Harris was particularly good with boys of fourteen and under and once again I was fortunate in having him as my first form master and then as the master that looked after Under-14 cricket. I was also in Thompson, so our paths crossed almost every day, for one reason or another.

I owe him a lot, not the least of which was the introduction and insight he gave me to English literature, to poetry and to the English language. Here were, suddenly, books that I had never heard of, adventure stories waiting to be read, the lilt of rhythm and rhyme of epic ballads in verse. No wonder that form prizes in the Prep. School centred round books like 'The Jungle Book' and 'Huckleberry Finn' and 'Wonder Tales from Many Lands'.

We also learnt, very quickly, team spirit; being part of a team, supporting that team. No individual, however big a part he played in the team, was bigger than the team itself. The boy who was not particularly good, but tried hard, was as important as the star of the team. Everyone could play their part for the benefit of the team. It would have done to day's Prima Donnas of our sporting world a lot of good if they had been in the Prep. School of Dunstable Grammar.

One of Mr. Harris's strictures was that in the summer term the Prep. would produce a play or an historical pageant on the lawn outside Ashton Lodge. Every boy would take part (the team spirit again), it was an educational part of the Prep's activities and it would have to be good, because it would be attended by proud mums and dads (well, mostly mums - it was an afternoon performance, only done once) together with younger brothers and sisters. But enjoyable also. And so it was

The Prep. School, summer term, forms I and II outside Ashtons Lodge. Mr C. L. Harris, centre. Waterlow's chimney can just be seen on the right.

really in the end, though Mr. Harris, whose brother was Christopher Fry, the play-wright, shook his head in despair on many occasions in the weeks and days that led up to THE DAY. Came the time on a warm summer's afternoon, with the audience sitting down one side on hard chairs, and frantic adjustments by the hard-working wardrobe mistress to some of the young actors' apparel, it all came right.

I remember two scenes in particular in which I was involved. The first occasion was when I was Captain Hook. I thought this was a wonderful part. Here I was in a pirate's outfit, with a black eye-patch and a red 'kerchief on my head, wielding a thin, silver painted wooden cutlass and stamping up and down, shouting away and making all sorts of terrible noises, as people were made to walk the plank. The only thing was that I got rather near the audience, in the front of which, sitting on the grass, were some of these little brothers and sisters. Such was the power of the cut-lass waving and the snarls and fearsome looks that were going on, that I'm afraid I made one little boy cry, he was so frightened. Well, there you are, there's nothing like playing a part successfully.

The second occasion was when I really did look the part, quite accidentally. This time we were enacting an English Pageant-through the-Ages type of production. The opening scene was one of Roman Britain. A young Briton would walk on look-ing about him as though he feared something. He would be pounced on by three Roman soldiers, a fight would ensue and he would then be dragged, struggling, to the Centurion, who would make a speech and mete out some unjust punishment. I was to be the young Briton.

Two days before the pageant was to take place I was allowed, by special dispensation for a Prep. School boy, to have my first cricket net. with the Shell forms. It was entirely my own fault that I was standing inside the net, where I should not have been, when I got hit by a cricket ball over the eye. There were a lot of stars shooting around suddenly and momentarily it knocked me out. I came to at the back of the net with Mr. H. J. Butters, that very fine master beloved by so many generations of boys (sometimes after they had left school when they had got over the feeling of 'Benjamin descending from on high' and fully realised his worth), standing over me. "Are you alright, lad?" he asked with concern. I nodded. 'Oh, good" he said "have a cherry", where upon he offered me an open bag of cherries that he had brought to the nets.

The result of this blow, of course, was a real shiner. I will leave aside the reaction of my mother when I got home and sheepishly walked into the kitchen, and jump two days to the pageant . By this time the colouring was at its best. It really was a very good black eye and it was realised, for those not in the know (i.e. the audience) that it could well be the result of a fight. So the scene was changed very slightly, there was a noise of a fight off-stage and I was dragged in, still fighting, until I fell to the ground in an appropriate place before the watching company. I was then hauled to my feet facing the audience before being marched to the Centurion. The result was quite good, really. Gasps went up, ladies' hands went to their mouths and the effect made me even prouder of my black eye than I was already (after all, it was my first one). I like to think that pageant got off to a realistic start . . . with the Wars of the Roses still to come. too.

I am not an actor, I never have been one and I had no burning desire to be one. but I did join the Dramatic Society after leaving the Prep. (Puck in Midsummer Night's Dream was my pièce de résistance) and on one notable occasion I was a girl pierrot. with three other 'girls', in an infamous Glee Club production in which other Dunstable folk joined. There was a strong bond between school and town and this concert, as part of the Golden Jubilee celebrations, was only one of many events, both at the school and in the town, where representatives of the two came together. over the years.

Certainly the town knew when anything special was on, aside from the normal coming and going of boys in term time to and from the school and up to the playing field and back, emphasised even more in High Street North (a bit like Waterlow's really, - there were set times when action took place and the streets were extra busy).

Speech Day was one of these special events when we were supposed to be on our best behaviour and to ensure that our clothes were especially clean (to some that was quite impossible). The whole school walked in a crocodile fashion up the High Street, down Church Street and into the Priory. The Rector took the service, the sermon was generally preached by a visiting clergyman, the headmaster and the head boy read lessons and the final hymn was always 'Jerusalem'. In the afternoon, prize-giving, preceded by the headmaster's report for the year. was generally held in the old Town Hall, though I also remember it in our own Speech Hall. On the platform were all the masters, wearing their gowns, the Governors (which included little white-haired Mr. Wallace, of carnation fame) and the visiting speaker. His obligatory request to the Head for a half-holiday raised the biggest cheer of the afternoon, but not necessarily the loudest noise. This was reserved, at the end. for the singing of the school song, a ballad-type composition written three years before the turn of the century and with a rousing tune and chorus, made all the more rousing by Mr. Leslie Boskett's rendering of it on the piano. It was a haunting school song, once sung, never forgotten. I used to put my heart and soul into the singing of this and I was not alone. not by the proverbial long chalk.

If the sound of that song was heard well outside the Town Hall, in the High Street and through the cross roads, then the noise of boys cheering on the School 1st XV at a rugger match on the playing field, tucked away between West Parade and West Street, also reverberated around in no uncertain manner.

The philosophy of Dunstable Grammar School about sport was quite simple. Unless you were excused it on genuine medical grounds, you played it. And if you were not playing in the match yourself on a Wednesday or a Saturday afternoon,

The cast of 'A Midsummer Night's Dream'. Puck seems to have one ear flap up and one ear flap down. It was written of his performance that he 'seemed to enjoy thouroughly his elfin pranks'. No further comment.

The Pierrot Troupe. Mr. Coales, left at the back and Mr. Boskett, far right are the two masters present. In the centre, seated, is Florrie Perry, who played a great part in musical circles in and around Dunstable, both in pre and post-war years, and guided and helped a whole host of young people. She often assisted at school concerts, taking the soprano lead, particularly for the Glee Club performances in the Easter term.

A performance by the Glee Club, in the Speech Hall. The stars in the front row include Mr. C. L. Harris and Mr. W. D. Coales. Old boys of pre-war vintage will also spot Messrs. Lack, Cadle, and Le Huray in the back row.

and there was a 1st XV rugby or a 1st XI hockey or cricket match at home, then in the senior school you supported that team and were expected to be present. Not expected, you had to be and house prefects would take a roll-call of the members of their house on the field to make sure you were there (and it was not just 100 lines if you were missing).

The school had a very fine reputation for the quality of its hockey, nurtured by H. J. Butters, who had played for his native Staffordshire and who turned out for School v Club matches at right back - heaven help any left-winger who tried to get the better of H.J.B., if the ball wasn't taken then that forward had shins much more sore than when he started the game. However, rugby lent itself to a more passionate reception than hockey, so when the rest of the school were watching the 1st XV a lot of passion was aroused off the field of play as well as on it. There were several times during the course of a game when those on the touchline let out a great, baying 'Scho-o-o-o-l' at the top of their voices, letting it go on for several minutes. When the 1st XV pack was encamped near their opponents' goal line, the word 'heel' got the same treatment. This sound swelled out of the ground to West Street on one side and down West Parade on the other, over the back streets of Princes, Victoria and Edward and down to High Street North itself. So in Dunstable there was no doubt what was going on when that noise was heard. There were two special event days in which townsfolk participated by coming to watch. Although the playing field was private property the big wooden gates in West Street, where cars could be driven in, and the little iron gate in West Parade, which was the common entrance for all members of the school, were always open when matches and events were on and visitors were always welcome.

One of these events was Sports Day, which was the athletic meeting of the year - all the races from the 100 yard dash for the Prep. School right through the various ages and distances to the Senior mile, plus the high jump and the long jump. There was no room for the javelin or throwing the discus or other such events. All during the week heats were run, so that Sports Day really consisted of the finals, unless wet weather caused a few semi-finals to be run also. It was a busy scene, taking place on a Saturday afternoon early in the summer term and the field was full of participants, time-keepers, parents and visitors with order always coming out of what could have been chaos. This was where a few of the masters who were not really all that interested in sport took an invaluable part - time-keeping, marshalling and generally organising. It meant that those masters who were in charge of XIs and XVs through out the school could be in the background and enjoy the scene, taking the opportunity too, to talk to parents and their friends. I took part in Sports Day, but to little effect. However, a boy was also running for his house, not just for individual glory, so points could be notched up here and there which could make all the difference to winning the House Cup or not.

The other big event was the Old Boys' Cricket Match on the last Saturday of the summer term and therefore right at the end of the school year. This, to me, was a big day, long before I had the privilege of playing in it and not just because of the fact that the long summer holidays lay ahead, although that meant, in turn, no more maths, no more chemistry, no more physics (my apologies to all those responsible for those subjects) and the yearly exams over. True, there was THE REPORT still to come and be opened, but with a bit of luck there would be some plus marks to outweigh the minuses that undoubtedly would be there.

After morning school on that Saturday of the Old Boys' Match, nearly every boy in the school took a chair from the Speech Hall up to the ground and encircled the field with them. Apart from a couple of benches and the seats within the pavilion enclosure itself, which were obviously reserved, there was no seating on the ground and with the whole school there (at least until the tea interval), Old Boys, parents, masters and wives, well-wishers, it was very necessary.

It was a happy scene, enhanced by the nature of the match itself. I would hold the big boys of the 1st XI, from the Sixth Form and the Upper Fifth, in awe and watch their progress keenly; cheer when an Old Boy's wicket fell but applaud also when a boundary was hit by those returning. Such was the balance of the game of cricket for me, even at an early age. In some way the game itself had got through to me, what it was really all about. I remember one particular stroke from an Old Boy (one who had made his mark in minor counties cricket for Buckingham shire) one year that brought every spectator on the ground to his or her feet. It was a straight six hit clean through the top window of a house in West Parade and it left a round hole just the size of a cricket ball. There was no other shattering of glass at all. The ground itself, as a cricket ground, was a good-sized one and that ball had to cover a good distance. There was, of course, an immediate rush of small boys to the boundary hedge to view the damage and the poor umpire, as the boys were right behind the wicket, was kept busy for a moment clearing them away.

There was another instance that stays in the memory, this in the 1938 special Golden Jubilee match against the M.C.C. - the school fast bowler, who was already playing for Bedfordshire, bowling the captain of Northants first ball. "Poetry in motion poetry in motion" his bowling was described to me by one of his team-mates in much later years. I am also told that when the same fast bowler removed the Reverend gentleman who was captain of the M.C.C. that day - and who was good enough to have opened for England some ten years earlier - the last ball before tea, the Reverend gentleman uttered a four-letter word, heard clearly as far as cover-point, that was not generally heard on the playing field of Dunstable Grammar School in those days . . . or any school playing field, come to that!

The School field - The Mill Field of old - was an enchanting place for me, in summer. I loved being up there at any time, in all terms, watching in the younger days, then mostly playing, particularly when I got into the 'Under 14' games and then matches. Suddenly, there was another wide-ranging aspect in life and I used to crowd into the passage way between the Speech Hall and the Quad, where the notice boards were, to see if I had been selected for the next match. The day was made if I had, even with a double maths period to come or the unequal struggle with Latin verbs an immediate prospect.

I knew very little outside Dunstable, really. We had no car, and holidays away at the sea were very few and far between. It was walking or catching a bus to walk and picnic somewhere. The only place I came to know well was by making friends, through our church, with a boy who came from Bury St. Edmunds and quite often after the initial 'allowed to go away by myself', I would spend some days with him in that East Anglian town. So to suddenly be a member of a team, to represent the school and be taken to matches in one of Mr. Costin's coaches, was a great experience. Thus we went to play at Luton Modern, The Cedars, St. George's Harpenden, Hitchin G.S., Bedford Modern, Caldicott, Wellbury Park and later at Aldenham, Berkhamsted, Royal Masonic Bushey, RCTS Pinner, Christ's College Finchley.... But naturally, it is the home field that one remembers. I must have played there hundreds and hundreds of times; I must have walked up there well over a thousand times. I was exceedingly lucky that I lived so close to the school itself. I literally just had to walk out of the shop in the morning, cross over the road and some fifty yards further on I was there. (However, I can remember three other boys who lived even closer). So to the playing field was only a five-minute walk. Along from the shop, up Union Street, along Victoria Street, past one side of Mr. Robinson's nurseries, up the alley and into West Parade. Or a variation thereof. When I was not playing myself there was often a call at a little sweet shop on the corner of Princes

Street and West Parade. This was owned by a Mrs. Dixon (sister-in-law to our Mr. Dixon, next door) and the shop had been converted from the front room of the house. Mrs. Dixon was a white-haired lady with a high-pitched voice who always wore a pinafore and was another person who always appeared from the back, when the shop door clanged. Her husband, 'Speedy' Dixon, used to walk round Dunstable at a very slow pace selling flowers that he had bought at Robinson's nurseries.

The Mill Field was an open field, but it also enjoyed seclusion, bounded as it was by the large terraced houses of West Parade and the brick wall of the back gardens of the houses in West Street at either end; the mill itself in one corner; two corner, small spinneys of trees; hedges and gardens and a line of trees, in the middle of which was the long jump run, by the side of the pavilion. Behind that pavilion ran the path known as Leighton Gap, a short cut between West Street and West Parade, where it came out alongside Miss Gurney's dress shop. Leighton Gap was also bordered by a black corrugated fence, behind which lay Mr. Seamons' extensive nurseries, with their greenhouses. Dunstable had a lot of nurseries for a small town, as besides those belonging to Mr. Robinson and Mr. Seamons there were five others in the Downs Road/Blows Road/ Borough Road area, one in Church Street, two in Chiltern Road and Mr. Larking in Victoria Street, at the top of Clifton Road, which we also used to go to. Of all those only one in Chiltern Road remains.

So with the open but enclosed nature of the ground it was almost free from the cold winds and the fresh breezes that I seem to have experienced since, standing on school playing fields, particularly Berkhamsted. The ground looked its best in summer, with all the changing shades of green and also because there was an uninterrupted view, with no rugby posts or hockey goals, anywhere.

The pavilion was not a big one, but like the school itself it had character and it blended in with the ground. It was, in fact, a very simple one, not designed to be grandiose by having a balcony and upstairs facilities and changing rooms all over the place and tables where thirty or so people could sit down to eat. It had width rather than depth and a sloping tiled roof with windows all along the front. It had one large middle room, with a wooden floor, which looked out on to the ground and where tea could be served in a buffet fashion in the summer. On one side was the changing room (where very little changing took place, boys and visiting sides walked up from the school in their playing kit and walked back down again, mud and all) which disappeared into obscure toilets and on the other a little room where tea could be prepared and where the tea urns were stored. Outside the main room was a small covered-in sitting area and then an enclosure of grass before the wooden pavilion railings. It was all very delightful sitting or standing in and around that pavilion and I never lost the thrill of going down the wide concrete path in the middle to play for the school at rugger, or with a hockey stick in my hand, wearing the chocolate and blue shirt, or walking out to bat. I don't think any of the Old Boys did, otherwise they would not have come back, from near and far, to play in the special matches of each term.

A summer afternoon, the pavilion.

The pavilion had two other attributes. Around the walls of the main room were ranged the photographs of all the school cricket 1st XIs going back some considerable way. Some were faded, some of the names difficult to read, but we looked at those photos over and over again. They had some kind of magnetic appeal. So we would find the lad who had had six seasons in the 1st XI, we would find fathers who now had sons there, we would find uncles and in my case a brother-in-law, we would find names and faces that were not of English extraction, we would find the well-known names. We searched in vain for Gary Cooper (obviously not a cricketer). We wondered whether our photographs would be there, in years to come. Little did we know....

The other attribute was more mundane. In the little tea room there was a hatch that in the summer, on school match days, was opened so that the watching boys could avail themselves of something to drink. Not tea, of course, but bottles of pop. So there were a few crates of Tizer and drinks like fizzy lemonade and American Cream Soda. After all, watching and playing around a bit in the nearby spinney and behind the high jump pit was thirsty work. It was well patronised by the younger boys and to have a few pennies in the pocket to share a bottle with two or three friends, for each of us to have a swig now and again, wiping the top with our hands when we had done so, was part of the enjoyment of the afternoon.

(I should think by now that the impression will have been given that, what with 'Daddy' Barnes' shop, Mrs. Dixon's shop and this last one in the pavilion we ate a considerable number of sweets and drank a lot of pop. Probably quite right. It was possible, actually, for a boy to buy something during mid-morning break at the official school tuck-shop near the Masters' Common Room, presided over by the inimitable Sergeant-Major Odell, make his second purchase of the day as he left the school gates with Mr. Barnes, pick up the odd item from Mrs. Dixon and finish off by the pavilion. Some did just that).

Very occasionally, now, if I happen to go along West Parade or along Leighton Gap, I stop and look across that same field, because it is still there, although there are differences. Over by the mill, there are now houses backing on to the field and along that side there are changes. There is no longer any entrance in West Street, more buildings stand on that stretch. The little wooden score box, over the other side opposite the pavilion and which had many initials carved into the thick wooden flap where the scorers placed their books, has gone - quite understandably, as it was somewhat decrepit. The big shed by the pavilion, which housed the mowers and all the sporting equipment and the pavilion itself have gone, that favourite pavilion, which is inexcusable - let go by the educational authorities so that in the end it had to be pulled down. It should have been a listed building, that pavilion, not one to be disregarded and let fall into disrepair.

The field looks forlorn, the boys have gone. And yet, for me, a hundred ghosts flit to and fro. I can see the scenes of yesteryear, I can hear the voices of days gone by. Where are they all, now, those friends? The Second World War scattered them and some did not return, one of whom I particularly remember and who lived but a hundred yards away from where I stand. And those who did come back? One is in Australia, one in Canada, one in the United States. They are in Devon, in Cornwall, in East Anglia, in Yorkshire, in Worcestershire, in Derbyshire, in Sussex, in Kent, in Cheshire and Lancashire, in Dorset, in the length and breadth of the land. Some of them are known, others I know not where. Not for me, I am afraid, not for any of us, really, will I be able to say . . .

> 'I will hold my house in the high wood
> Within a walk of the sea,
> And the men that were boys when I was a boy
> Shall sit and drink with me.'

No chapter on the Grammar School that I remember can be written without talking about the masters, because nearly all of them had some influence on me and the time I spent at this school was after all a large and important chunk of my early life in Dunstable. All of them, knowingly or perhaps unknowingly, set the pattern that whatever is taken out of life, in any walk, something must be put back. Theirs was a philosophy that with the greatest respect, all teachers of the young would do well to follow today~ in these apparently turbulent times of education.

Some masters I knew better and came into contact with more than others, simply because they were my form master, or house master, or the master in charge of a particular XI or XV. I have already spoken of Mr. Harris and referred to Mr. Butters, both of whom played an important part in my education. But no mention of H. J. Butters can really do justice to the man. He taught geography, which I enjoyed, he was the P.T. master and he was the master in charge of games. His house was at the West Parade corner of the playing field by the little gate. He was a strict disciplinarian and no boy, if he had the slightest grain of common sense in him, ever tried to get the better of H.J.B. You could get away with things, sometimes, with two or three other masters, but not Mr. Butters.

He was the first to encourage a boy who had no outstanding talents. And he had a kind and understanding heart, particularly if he knew you were doing your best. He understood, for example, that a young boy batting in the cricket nets, facing a hard straight ball coming down fast, had a general tendency to back away to leg. He had a simple remedy. A bucket of water was placed immediately behind the legs. That cured the habit fast, and no-one lost face. Coming from Staffordshire, Mr. Butters naturally tended to support Stoke City F.C. From an early term, he knew my affinity to Arsenal. I think he was slightly amused at my depth of feeling, but I think also that he thought, well, here's a boy who has a great love and support for his team and is not likely to be swayed and therefore should not be looked at lightly. Anyway, he said one day that if ever Stoke City had their away fixture against Arsenal in the holidays, he would take me to see the match. Three years later they did and I reminded him politely of the conversation. There was no deliberation whatever; there was an instant reply. "Right", he said "off we go". So we did. He took me up on the train from Luton, we watched the game at Highbury, standing on the terraces on a bitterly cold December day and he then treated me to a hot meal at a restaurant somewhere off Piccadilly Circus before returning home. Arsenal won 4 - 0, yes, but I didn't remember that day for the result alone....

The third of the masters with whom I had a lot to do was Mr. Bancroft - F.M.B. A Welshman of true Welsh fervour, but not overdoing it, he was the senior history master, taught divinity and, as I came through the school, the master in charge of rugby and cricket. I enjoyed history and, being brought up to go to church, divinity did not bore me. Mr. Bancroft was a big man in every way and another strict disciplinarian but, again, kind and understanding. He was also the sort of man that you could sit on the ground with, as I did, in the break in a rugger game on a late, warm September day and just have a chat. We were on the same wavelength Although he came to the school much later than Mr. Butters, Old Boys would often speak about Bancroft and Butters in the same breath.

I can recall many moments with Mr. Bancroft, including facing his two types of bowling - his innocent, beguiling slow spinners, tossed high in the air and his 'faster' stuff coming in from the West Street end with every fibre of his ample frame quivering. But there was one happening that I particularly remember, quite understandably, as will be appreciated.

If there were no matches on a Wednesday afternoon in the summer term then the 1st XI and the 2nd XI would join forces to play a full game between themselves. It was properly scored and was invaluable practice out in the middle as distinct from having nets (which we had twice a week, in any case). It so happened, on that particular afternoon, that, batting first I scored runs and was not out, with another batsman also, when we came in. Any boy, playing cricket, wants to know how many runs he has scored if he has had a reasonable innings. We never knew our individual total, as there was nowhere to put it up, so I asked the scorer when he wandered over from the little box. "97" was the reply, which Mr. Bancroft happened, by chance, to overhear. There was an instant decision, although no action was really necessary at all. "Come on, everybody", F.M.B. called out, "out again, quick, as we were". He made everyone come out on to the field of play again, before the other side's innings began, so that I had the chance of getting the other three runs, which, thank goodness, I did. It was not all that important, really, it was not a match against another school that would be recorded in history, but Mr. Bancroft knew what it would mean to a schoolboy and gave him that opportunity.

Then there was W. D. Coales ('Codey') second master and occupier of the chemistry laboratories. Mr. Coales was chemistry and chemistry was Mr. Coales. Many are the tales told about his chemistry experiments. A feature at the school, seemingly since it first began, he was an active man, very quick on his toes. He took part in the aforementioned Glee Club concert and brought the house down with his spirited rendering of 'I made 'em do the cake walk'. No record of the Grammar School would ever be complete without him, his contribution was considerable.

Where Mr. Coales invented chemistry, so to speak, Wilfred Lack lived in the physics laboratory, close by. He had a little room in the corner of that lab. and no-one quite knew what was in it. From time to time he would disappear there. Rumour and counter rumour abounded but the puzzle was never satisfactorily solved. Mr. Lack was also in charge of the swimming pool and of swimming. He was a man of many parts, doing a great number of things around the school, including teaching woodwork. He is forever immortalised for his nickname ('Fudger') and for his drawing of a dotted line on the blackboard. He would draw an ordinary line, wet his finger and then make breaks in the chalk. Mr. Lack, later on, gave great service to the town, becoming the Mayor of Dunstable, an Alderman and the holder of an O.B.E. He was always willing to help in special events, both at the school and in the town. The old Dunstable Borough Council, in due course, gave him the honour of Alderman Emeritus.

Leslie Boskett (the same Mr. Boskett of 'The Square') was the senior maths master as well as a brilliant pianist and a fearless hockey umpire. His opening phrase at any lesson, in his own dialect, was "Now, now, boys" and he had the extraordinary habit, when taking a new piece of chalk from the cupboard, of breaking off the top and tossing it with unerring accuracy out of one of the top windows of the tall classroom. He was thus known as 'Toss' and there were times when we used to hide the used chalk in order to see this performance carried out. He, too, took part in much activity in Dunstable, participating in concerts all over the place as well as being the organist every Sunday for the church. He was a great organiser. I am grateful to him, amongst other things, for getting me through School Certificate Algebra, which he ought to have ranked as one of his outstanding achievements.

Freddie Cadle was a quiet man and I suspect under-rated in his value to the school. A bachelor who lived at Ashton Lodge in term time, he was the second master in Thompson House, his main subject Latin, although he took English as well. He always carried into any class a knobbly, short stick, and a cardboard, open file of papers which bulged outwards and always seemed likely to fall out all over the place. He used to walk around making music in his head and he was a writer of fairy stories. When I was confined to my bedroom at home for a month with scarlet fever, Mr. Cadle wrote out the whole instructions for me as to how to play Patience,

The Science Block, built in 1907.

The Chemistry Laboratory, the domain of the mercurial Mr. Coales.

which was no mean feat, in order to help me pass the time. On the more active side Mr. Cadle played and looked after Fives and I had much pleasure, on a Friday afternoon, playing this fascinating and exhausting game in one of.the two Rugby Fives courts in the quad, at the side of the swimming pool.

Like Mr. Cadle, Fred Speke hailed from Gloucestershire and was another quiet man, but totally dedicated and very much liked. Coming three years after I had started, our paths never crossed all that much as house and form and year of teaching did not meet, but when I did talk with him I found again we were on the same wavelength. Many years later an Old Boy, whom I didn't know really, said to me that one of his outstanding memories of the school was Mr. Speke and the help he gave this boy in his attempt to swim. The boy found it difficult, but persevered and when at long last he managed a length of the baths, "Do you know", said the Old Boy, "Mr. Speke was so pleased he gave me a shilling".

Mr. A. C. Wadsworth, of the precise English voice, was the epitome of an English gentleman. He taught English, too, amongst other subjects, but he is probably best remembered as the producer of some excellent school plays and for being the head of the school Cadet Corps. Although not specifically under the control of Mr. Wadsworth, but with his support and liaison, the Corps, with invaluable assistance from Old Boys, had a very fine drum and bugle band, which paraded at church services throughout the year, on Speech Day and at special civic services and events. where they were much in demand, as well as participating in tournaments outside the county. They were a stirring sight and sound, marching through the town and at the end giving an 'eyes right' salute to the school as they reached it on the way back. Mr. Wadsworth also owned a little Austin Seven car, which he parked in the school quad and which was the object of schoolboy pranks on more than one occasion. Like Mr. Lack he was also to be honoured and received the M.B.E.

Little Mr. Le Huray, the Channel Islander who made his home in Dunstable, was the German master - ironic that he should teach the language of the nation that was to occupy his homeland; he had a shock of grey hair, a little, bristling moustache and walked with his feet at forty-five degrees. M. Poirier, the French master (there is often one master in a school that a boy does not get on with - M. Poirier and I did not see eye to eye). 'Badger' Brock from Wales who often questioned, with suitable action, the mental stability of the boy he was talking to and who was failing to comprehend; he lies in the peace and quiet of Totternhoe churchyard. Mr. Hedges, part-time 'Singing' master, taking lessons in the Lecture Room, with its ascending rows of benches and with the boys bellowing out sea shanties and songs from a Boosey & Hawkes cloth book, as well as hymns that we would be singing at morning assembly. The tall and elegant Miss Draper, a Victorian lady who dwelt amongst us twice a week for Art lessons.

All these masters were under the headship of Mr. A.F.R. Evans, who, although I saw him daily, at assembly and also at school home matches, I never knew well. To me he was a man aloof, but having said that I know he ran an efficient school and his staff were very loyal to him. I am sure he knew much more about me than I did of him.

The Common Room, 1938
*From left to right: **back row:** F. R. Speake, F. M. Bancroft, R. L. Poirier, A. C. Wadsworth, W. N. Brock, F. Cadle*
__Seated:__ C. L. Harris, L. A. Boskett, W. D. Coales, A. F. R. Evans, (Headmaster), H. J. Butters, C. P. Le Huray.

Speech Day in the old Town Hall, the Headmaster - Mr A. F. R. Evans - presiding. A 1937 scene.

On the last day of the school year, one summer, after our final assembly and with everybody departing I was crossing the almost deserted quad. Over by the memorial library there was a lad, who was in the Upper Fifth, quietly crying. He was a boy who had been somewhere in the middle of the class, not particularly good at games and who had left no outstanding mark on his school life. But he was well liked. Mr. Bancroft was trying to comfort him. "What's the matter,—?" he said. The boy dried his eyes, smiled a wan smile and replied . . . "I'm leaving today, sir. I don't want to leave. I've been so happy here".

Part of the War Memorial Library, around 1930, given to the school by Old Dunstablians' Club in memory of those pupils killed in the Great War.

43

The School from the Quad. The nearest five first-floor windows were the dormitories for the boarders. The large window on the right, at the edge of the photograph, part of the Library.

Chapter Six

The War and After

The war did not officially begin until 1939, but the autumn of 1938 was clouded with apprehension, only to be replaced by the spurious confidence engendered by the Munich agreement.

There were two features of this time. The Rugby XV was the School's best ever. It played 9 matches, winning 8 and drawing the other, with a points total of 248 for and 32 against. In all, the School Rugby teams played 24 matches, winning 19, drawing 1 and losing 4. Then there was a splendid Boarders' Reunion Dinner, destined to be the last, attended by Mrs. Thring and E. E. Apthorp. A brief summer, and we were at war. We as a school were fortunate not to have a major disruption of staff, most of whom were beyond the age at which school masters were required to serve, but with Air Raid Warden duties, Fire Watching, Home Guard and A.T.C. there was plenty to be done at home. The task of those who remained behind was to keep the school going as normally as possible and to maintain the highest possible standards. School numbers continued to increase—this was considered a reasonably safe area — and we soon topped the 300 mark. By this time we were entering regularly some 8 or 10 candidates for Higher School Certificate, and though, as the war progressed, Universities were almost closed, we prepared a number of candidates for University careers when the opportunity permitted.

Wartime Prize Giving Day, 1942.

Apart from the Cadet Corps activities, this school has never had any particular military association. The majority of our boys who joined up attached themselves to the local regiment or to the new service, the R.A.F. The former were unfortunate in being drafted to the Far East where many of them arrived in time for the surrender to the Japanese at Singapore. Several died in prison camps, others survived their horrors. Those who joined the R.A.F. suffered heavily in the earlier years when our forces were still building their strength. By the end of the war a further 45 names were available for the School's Honours List.

Upper-Fifth formers on a day-out to Bedford, 1940s.

Amid the flurry of war R.S.M. Odell died in 1941 and E. E. Apthorp in 1942. In 1943 the Headmaster was away ill for a whole term; W. D. Coales acted as a most capable deputy. It was in this year that people began to think of a time after the war, and in November plans were prepared for the creation of an Old Dunstablians' Memorial Fund, to provide assistance for the education of the children of Old Boys killed in the war and to assist Old Boys who might have fallen on hard times. This was felt to be a fitting and practical memorial; the scheme itself was the inspiration of H. J. Butters. In the event the Education Act of 1944 was to render some of the scheme's provisions unnecessary, but the idea was an imaginative one and the funds have been put to many useful if rather different ends for those originally anticipated. I am sure they would have met with H. J.'s. approval.

Six years of war slipped quickly by as a dream. When V. E. Day came there was everywhere a feeling of extreme thankfulness: the most riotous thing to do was to switch on all the lights and draw back the curtains. Gradually our absentees returned in time for the General Inspection of 1946, delayed on account of the war. The Inspectors found us a happy school; we even put on a Cricket match for their delectation, J. A. Fendley won an Open Scholarship in Natural Science to Oriel College, Oxford. He was later to gain one of the best Firsts of his year. H. M. Hayward gained his First in Modern Languages at Magdalen College, Oxford, and was appointed a Tutor of the College. M. F. W. Lack won a Naval Cadetship to Dartmouth, and 9 boys were successful in the Higher School Certificate examination. Speech Day of that year was notable for the disclosure that in consequence of the Education Act previously mentioned the School would no longer have Direct Grant status but would come completely under the control of the Local Authority. The Preparatory Department would soon cease to exist, but the Boarding House would continue. In view of the changes this would make in school life it was decided to form the first year entry boys into their own Junior House. H. J. Butters was placed in charge, assisted, as the Preparatory Department declined, by J. G. Matthewman. This first year was to be one of preparation for an introduction into the life of a Grammar School, and the arrangement has continued happily to this day.

War Weapons Week Parade, 1942.

In the summer of 1948 came the news that A. F. R. Evans proposed to retire after twenty one years as Headmaster. His stay at the school was marked by continuing progress. He had done his share in adding to and improving the School buildings, notably in being responsible for the completion of the Memorial Library; during his time the number of boys in attendance at school had almost doubled, and a new level of success in public examinations had been achieved. He had, too, the quality of friendship, of complete loyalty to his friends and to his staff. He retired at the time of transition from the Direct Grant to the Local Authority sphere, believing it best that his successor should start from the beginning of the new regime, and departed to the West Country to enjoy his motoring and his fishing. He died in 1960, quite suddenly, as he would have wished. A modest, quiet man, and a great gentleman.

****

ANOTHER VIEW OF THE CADET CORPS 1938 - 1947
by Roger Hazell

Leaving the Prep School for the REAL SCHOOL had many advantages, one of which I clasped to my bosom with the enthusiasm of youth. I could apply to join the (O.T.C.) Cadet Corps. The cost to my parents was but a few shillings for a baton stick and brass-cleaning wadding.

In retrospect, I believe I was motivated by a latent wish to be an actor; for one night a week, I could exchange my dark jacket, grey shorts and Eton collar for the instantly recognisable uniform of a potential hero - a real khaki uniform! To my amazement, my request to join was accepted without qualification and with marked enthusiasm, so in no time I was kitted out in a complete Beds & Herts Regiment World War I uniform from cap to puttees, and bore the proud legend, in brass, on my epaulettes, "Dunstable School". My mother did not shed a tear, though I suspect my father probably did

We "played" at soldiers, we drilled, we learned words of command, we engaged the Hun on maps, and then real War broke out. I believe to the hundred or so of us, it passed unnoticed until the day we exchanged our uniform for battle dress, and our title from O.T.C. to Army Cadet Force; Sandhurst was obviously meant for greater mortals. For my part, I had now risen to be Lance Corporal.

Our training became a little more realistic in that we carried out field exercises in the summer, crawling around Sewell Farm and Dunstable Sewage Works, throwing thunderflash bangers as hand grenades, and letting off "crackerblank" as small arms fire. We were issued with First Aid manuals, which provided a fairly explicit chapter on delivering babies. I do not recall anyone asking if, when, where, or why we should be carrying out this task.

For many of us the next hurdle was obtaining the qualification entitled "War Cert.A". This was awarded as the result of a Part I and Part II examination. Part I was fairly easy and involved a knowledge of flag signals, drilling a platoon, and the exercise of stripping modern weapons such as the sten machine carbine and/or Bren gun into its component parts and reassembling it in working order. For the latter, the examining officer would find himself a suitable site such as the armoury, the bike sheds, or in my case, the entrance to the air raid shelter. At his advanced age, modern weaponry was a complete mystery to him, so he devised the simple expedient of making the first candidate strip the weapon, the second assemble it, and so on. On reflection, it was probably fortunate for many of us that we were totally unaware of the procedure, for had the case been otherwise, then I feel convinced that one candidate would have made off with a vital part of the dismantled weapon, leaving both the next candidate and the adjudicating officer in an embarrassed state.

By the time I reached the rank of Corporal, I had decided that despite Hitler's decision to leave me alone and capture a few Russian lads instead, I had had enough. However, before I could summon up courage to make my intention known, War Cert A Part II was upon me. So there we were answering questions on map reading, lines of fire (or was it fields of fire?), and nothing on childbirth, and doing quite well, despite the old chestnut questions of what is the weight of a pull through, to which the answer is, "The brass weight at the end," and not, "About 1 - 2 ounces,"when I was struck a mortal blow by being taken into the countryside and led by the R.S.M to meet an extremely elderly Brigadier who must have fought as a youth with General Gordon. "See that hill over there?" he said, pointing a withered finger in the direction of a small knoll in the middle of an enormous field, whilst beating his begartered right leg with his baton "The enemy are up there, and you are here with your platoon to flush the beggars out - eh?" My platoon, like his enemy, were total figments of our individual imaginations, for there were only the three of us by the hedge, viewing the tranquil Summer scene. I was not totally nonplussed by all of this, for we had been through such imaginary games many a time before. The whole ploy was simple, or rather based on a simple premise: the enemy were always a cowardly bunch of brainless yokels, so provided one directed enough fire in their direction, they would react to rule and keep their heads down until you and your platoon could rush upon them to put them out of their misery with a bayonet. No one ever bothered to mention the simple fact that the accuracy of a Lee Enfield 0.303 rifle diminished by the power of 10 once a bayonet was fitted. However, this was not going to worry me or my phantom platoon. So the ploy was, two men on the Bren gun firing happily at the hill, whilst the eight riflemen crawled along a hedge to get closer to the enemy. Then the riflemen opened fire and the Bren gunners moved to another, closer, position, and so the leapfrog game continued until you were upon the enemy. So, as descriptively as possible, I spelt out each move to the Brigadier for some ten minutes whilst he nodded sagely.

I was then struck by two bare facts. Firstly, in this period of time my platoon would have fired more rounds than it was possible for them to carry, and more importantly, the last piece of cover was a good 100 yards from the summit. I faltered. "Come along, lad, the War can't wait, yer know!" I baldly stated, "Radio the RAF for a squadron of rocket firing typhoons". The R.S.M. dragged me away from the purple faced Brig, whispering in my ear, "You're a b.........fool, that's what you are!" (He would have had to add 'Sir' in the days of the O.T.C.) "You should have said, 'Charge up the hill!'" Protestations that this was the path to total annihilation of my "men" fell on deaf ears. I failed, I vowed to resign.Before I could do so, I was into a retake of part II and this time, on some different field, I left a mess which made the Somme look like a pub brawl, and was loudly congratulated on my initiative.

Chapter Seven

Changing Times

G. H. Bailey was appointed to succeed A. F. R. Evans. A Cambridge Rugby Blue, he came from King's College, Canterbury, where he had been Games Master and Housemaster. The appointment had been delayed, so that W. D. Coales again acted as Headmaster until Mr. & Mrs. Bailey arrived in January 1949.

He recalls many interesting memories of his stay, while emphasising the difficulty of being objective at such close range. "The years 1949-60 may be regarded by the historian as a period of transition in which a routine partly based on boarding life changed to that of the completely 'day' school. Certainly the boarding routine had been a strong feature, with its Saturday lessons and games, its Sunday services in the Priory Church, the school and immediate grounds open long into the evening, resident masters available for help and consultation. Conditions, however, were changing. Restrictions on entry to the Boarding House meant an inevitable decline in numbers, and eventually came the sad decision to close the House. Habits, however, died slowly — not least that for many the school was a living centre after the last lessons of the day or term were over. Even the controversial introduction of the five day week did not mean a Saturday "shut down", but with it came the full realisation that we were a 'day' school.

It had its compensations. With the growth of the town and the immediate neighbourhood came a bigger demand for entry. The boarding accommodation offered the necessary initial classrooms for a three form entry. All this time there was a demand for more teaching rooms. Some came. The 'temporary' classrooms erected on the old garden provided an Art room and a History room. The dormitories, though somewhat inconvenient and inaccessible, were adapted, one making a Geography room; the old Art-cum-Geography room became a much needed Biology laboratory."

The work and life of the school went on. Unfortunately, during these days two valuable members of the staff died. Although he did not die till 1950, H. J. Butters was truly a victim of the war years. All who remember him will know how wholeheartedly he threw himself into any venture he considered worth-while. In the Home Guard and as Commanding Officer of the local A.T.C. he was unsparing of his physical resources. We saw him decline gradually, until at the beginning of the Autumn term he quietly passed away.

The value of his work to the school over a period of 32 years was incalculable, and he was in every sense a man. His memory is perpetuated by the gift by an Old Boy, of the Butters Shield, awarded annually to a boy who, though having no innate ability, has by courage and determination made himself into a useful games player.

Dr. Ault spent 11 years in charge of French. He was a perfectionist, a man of high intellectual powers, who fought disease with enormous courage and spirit. To both of them death came as a friend; may the earth rest lightly on them.

In this period of change the life of the school went on busily. 1950 saw the revival of the Parents' Association, later to develop into the Parents-Staff Association. The parents as a body have done wonderful work for the school by personal service and by providing financial aid for the many school organisations. For many years they have provided teas on the school field and have catered for our needs at many school functions. Without their assistance the Duke of Edinburgh Award Scheme could not have been started. More recently they have given an organ for the Speech Hall, a cine camera with all equipment, and a film projector. They have asked nothing but to be allowed to help the school. Among those who have especially helped are Dr. Forsdyke, C. W. Gilder, G. Combes, W. Buckingham, A. G. K. Ball, J. Stevenson, J. Powell, and J. G. Matthewman.

In 1951 W. T. Lack succeeded W. D. Coales as Second Master, the latter having reached retirement age, though he remained for another eight years in charge of Science. In the same year A. F. Towell, who served on the staff for several years played for England v. Scotland at Twickenham. In 1952 the first school camp since the war was held in Snowdonia, the precursor to many school trips and camps since. 1951 and 1952 saw some wonderful Rugby by the school 1st XV, which won 23 out of 27 matches, scoring over 500 points in the process. When the Beds. County R.F.C. was formed with F. M. Bancroft as Chairman, we were to have several representatives in the sides, while we also contributed players to the Beds. Young Amateurs Cricket XI. A Garden Fete held at the School in 1953 realised a profit of £291. This was the result of a combined effort by the School, Parents and Old Boys. The parents now hold an annual bazaar in the Autumn term.

All this time educational standards were on the upgrade. The increasing prosperity of the district, the growing numbers in the school, the development of County Major Scholarships, were all important factors. In 1950 18 boys were successful in the Higher School Certificate examinations, 12 went on to Universities. 16 were successful in 1951 (by this time in the G.C.E. Advanced level examinations); 10 went on to universities. 20 passed 'A' level in 1952, 13 went to universities; G. Dolling won an Open Science Scholarship to Cambridge in 1954, later gaining 1st Class Honours; State Scholarships were gained annually, as many as 4 in 1952. The number of candidates for 'O' level grew from about 25 to past the 50 mark. In a few years 'A' level candidates were to be more than 30, 'O' level 70. We were now a three form entry school, and a move was made to create a fast moving stream of the more academically fitted boys. That it has been a limited success has been due to the necessity to make this a full rather than a part form. The School was honoured in 1956 by the election of W. T. Lack as Mayor of Dunstable, a position he was to fulfil with distinction for three years, his work being recognised by the award of the O.B.E.

*R.W.S. Smith, Chairman of Governors, makes a presentation to W.D.Coales
on his retirement, 1959.*

The last years of the fifties were to be more diffficult. These increases in numbers provided their own problems. The Medway Huts eased the classroom difficulty, but even with the adoption of a classroom into a Biology Laboratory space was desperately small. Speech Day had to be divided into two parts, Senior and Junior. It was quite impossible to accommodate all in the hall. Dr. Ault and L. A. Boskett were each away ill for long periods, and their places were difficult to fill. It was at this time that Dr. Ault died, and in the following months the long connection of W. D. Coales and L. A. Boskett with the school ended. Both had been connected with the school for 50 years, W. D. Coales as Science Master, and L. A. Boskett first as a pupil and then as Mathematics Master. Their long and devoted service has its own place in our annals. Then in the autumn of the year came the news that the Headmaster was to move to Wolverstone Hall School, near Ipswich. Both he and Mrs. Bailey were very attached to the ideals of the Boarding School, and this was an opportunity to take up again the threads of boarding school life. While we regretted their departure, we realised that they were making their own choice for the future. They left behind many friends, won by their easy, happy companionship.

G. H. Bailey was a man who gave his trust implicitly to those with whom he worked; dealing with boys he always tried, even in the worst, to find some quality of good to which he could appeal, and only rarely was he disappointed. He himself has summed up his stay here with these words: "I have always regarded the spirit and atmosphere of a school as vitally important. At Dunstable there was a happy co-operation between boys, staff, parents, the Old Boys, the Governors and the L. E. A. Particularly pleasant memories will long remain of the way in which all had the welfare of the school at heart."

It would not be fitting to close this chapter without a reference to two School Secretaries who served during the time. Increasing offfice work after the war led to the appointment of Miss Hazel Alabaster who retired from the post on her marriage to F. R. Speke. She was succeeded by Mrs. I. Williams. To both these ladies the school owes a considerable debt for their unfailing kindness and adaptability in all kinds of circumstances.

K.W.Nazimuddin, Prime Minister of Pakistan, inspects his old dormitory.

****

TEACHING IN THE FIFTIES
A conversation with J. Brennan

He remembers the relative formality of the Staff room in those days, with the older members of the staff invariably addressed as 'Mr. So and So'. Apparently, there was plenty of time for bridge and chess and for discussion of current affairs. As he was a member of the PE Staff, it was one of Mr. Brennan's duties to weigh and measure each new pupil as he came into school, and he remembers a class which contained a boy who weighed seventeen stones, and another who weighed three stone, ten pounds. Rugby, he recalls, was played throughout the Autumn term, and hockey from Christmas to Easter. In the summer, cricket and tennis were fitted around the demands of public examinations. Mr. Brennan recalls the quarter of an hour walk to West Parade for games, and the primitive changing facilities there.

One particular memory of Mr. Brennan's concerned some staff surveillance at the end of term when a person or persons unknown had added some potassium permanganate to the official contents of the school swimming pool. Staff members, in twos and threes, were keeping an undercover round the clock watch in the pool area, and Mr. Brennan and two colleagues were on the eleven o'clock "shift". They heard a suspicious "chinking" sound and were in time to apprehend a Waterlow's shift worker with a carrier bag, on a return trip from the local off licence.

P. M. Cleave

Chapter Eight

The Latest Age

Our new Headmaster, L. P. Banfield, M.A., and Mrs. Banfield came to us from Bromley Grammar School, where he had been first Deputy then Acting Headmaster. L. P. Banfield was educated at Chichester High School and Exeter College, Oxford. During the war he served in the Army in the S. E. Asia Command, retiring with the rank of Major. It is perhaps significant that he is the first of our Headmasters whose experience has been wholly that of day schools, and with the departure to Oxford of J. Thorogood, the last survivor of the Boarding House, the final link with boarding days has been severed.

During the three years of his consulship the Headmaster has made certain changes. Notably there has been an introduction of the new school uniform, with blazers of a consistent black instead of the rather varying colours of chocolate formerly in vogue. The status of Prefect has been enhanced by the wearing of short gowns, no mere gimmick but giving all boys the opportunity of recognising authority, a very valuable development in a school where alas! no longer does everyone know everyone else. The Parents' Association has become the Parents Staff Association and parents of boys of all ages now attend open evenings to meet the staff responsible for teaching their sons. At the moment of writing, Phoenix-like from the ashes of the old filter plant room and lavatories is rising a new building, and behind this a new Science Block as the first phase of a new building plan. W. D. Coales' vision of 1909 is being accomplished.

In the three years he has been here L. P. Banfield has already made his mark. He is above all insistent on the demand for high academic standards. The process of development we have traced earlier has continued; in the summer of 1962, 92 candidates took the 'O' level examinations, 42 the 'A' level. Twenty two boys went on to university, the school's highest performance to date. Old Boys and parents may well feel that in this latest age, in spite of change, the traditions of the school are being continued and strengthened.

****

56

THE FINAL YEARS
An Update by some Old Boys

At last the new science laboratories, promised for so many years, were completed and handed over in 1964! Mr. W.D.Coales, Senior Science Master until his retirement in 1959, unveiled a plaque on July 15th, Founder's Day, commemorating his fifty years' loyal service to the school and officially declaring the new science laboratories open.

Unveiling the Memorial Plaque at the new Science buildings, 1964.

A quote from the School Magazine of 1964 states "One of the problems of our time seems to be that of lack of communication." Under the leadership of the headmaster, Philip Banfield, a School Council was formed to attempt to bridge this gap. Its aim was to discuss and explain policies which must be implemented and to acquire some knowledge and understanding of the ideas of modern youth. A major proposal enacted by the School Council, which comprised both masters and pupils, was to revitalise the existing House System. This was achieved by reducing the number of Houses from four to three. The new House Names were Ashton, a school name, Bedford, a local name and Churchill, a national name. Shell forms were included in the system, and each House divided into three sections, Senior, Middle and Junior. Academic, sport and cultural activities were all taken into account, based on a comprehensive points table devised and run by Mr. R.H.Symes, to determine "Cock House." The need for religion was also recognised and arrangements put into place for House Prayers to be held every fortnight.

Recipients at Annual Prizegiving, 1967.

The retirement of Mr.W.T. Lack in 1965 ended another long association between school and master. He served both school and the local community faithfully for many years and was fondly remembered by all with whom he had been associated.

Two years later Mr. J.D.B.Milne retired after 23 years service, teaching 'O' level maths in the classroom and rugby on the playing field. In extra curricular activities the Chess Club in particular owed him a debt of gratitude.

Academic and sporting achievements continued to improve year on year, which reflected the hard work put in by both staff and pupils.

In 1971 Dunstable Grammar School finally closed its doors for the last time, giving way to the new comprehensive system of education.

****

L.P. BANFIELD

1960 - 1971 - a retrospective

My first recollection of the Grammar School (apart from the interview for the Headship, which took place in what I was later to discover was my own dining room) was on Good Friday 1960. We had moved up from London the previous day and I felt sufficiently settled in to go through the connecting door from the School House to the Head's study, where, feeling fairly proud of my achievement, I sat at the imposing desk. Casually I opened the main drawer - to discover it had no bottom! The difference between shadow and substance was ominous.

The facade of the buildings facing the High Street was impressively Victorian but inside things were less awe-inspiring. The fabric had worn badly and had clearly not been respected as it should have been. Facilities such as specialist rooms hardly existed. The Science Laboratories were inadequate and old fashioned. (I fancied I could see ALCHEMY written over the door of the Chemistry Lab.) In the Sixth Form room, immediately over the boiler house, teachers had the alternative of keeping the windows closed and being suffocated, or having them open and being unable to make themselves heard above the roar of traffic from the High Street.

I ask myself what gives me most satisfaction as I look back to those years. I had felt instinctively when I arrived that the pace of academic study was too leisurely, with the result that all except the very well motivated boys tended to under-achieve. Sixth formers felt it was necessary to stay for a third year to obtain a University place. While this was very good for the Rugger and Cricket teams, which tended to be very mature indeed, it was rather a waste of resources. So I take pride in the fact that examination results showed a steady improvement over the years. The 28 'A' level candidates who in 1960 collected only 44 passes gave way to the 51 in 1969 who gained 156. The 1960 'O' level entry which averaged only 4 passes apiece, gave way to the 1967 entry which averaged 7. The numbers staying on in the Sixth Form approached 75% of our intake; the same proportion of those went on to Higher Education.

But there was much more cause for pride. The traditional Cock House Competition, based on four Houses named after distinguidshed former members of staff, had stagnated. In response to the suggestions of the elected School Council (itself an innovation) a new system was set up of three Houses and the range of activities covered considerably extended to include much more than the traditional Games, including academic achievement. This last was assessed according to some mysterious points system which only Mr Symes (who controlled it) understood!

To celebrate the seventy-fifth anniversary of the School's foundation we set ourselves a target of raising a four figure sum for the Freedom from Hunger campaign, which finally totalled £1500, a considerable sum in pre-inflation days.

One of the most valuable means of character building lay at hand in the Duke of Edinburgh Award Scheme. The school was a pioneer in this scheme under the leadership of Mr Bancroft and involved a considerable number of boys who regularly gained awards at all levels.

In spite of poor facilities, the Dramatic Society mounted some impressive productions. Over all our activities there was always tremendous help and support from the Parents Staff Association.

The school regularly fielded six teams for all the major games on Saturdays. The General Elections of 1964 and 1966 heralded changes in the organisation of education in the county, and after a never-to-be forgotten cliff-hanging debate by the County Council, the present scheme was finally ratified. There followed a period of frenzied activity, during which we all tried to prepare ourselves for the impending changes - wide-ranging discussions carried out with mutual toleration for our naturally differing views while we sought to ensure that what we should offer in our new role should be, at least, as good as in the old one.   On reflection, Kenneth Baker might have learned a good deal had he sat in with us!

As we were about to become co-educational, I asked that our last selective intake in 1971 should be a mixed one, so that when we moved to the present site, we did in fact have some 39 girls in the first year, together with four Sixth Form girls. The Staff, which had not been wholly male in the past, now received several additional ladies as colleagues.

The move to Caddington followed. A brief note in the Log Book records that on Monday July 26, 1971, the Headmaster and School Secretary established their administration in the new school.

Chapter Nine

Games and Societies

There are many activities which do not appear on the School time table which are, nevertheless, essential to the well being of the school and its inhabitants. Some mention has already been made of the importance of school games. For thirty years, W. F. Brown ran the School Cricket, ably assisted by E. E. Apthorp. J. B. Escolme was a tremendous soccer enthusiast, while W. E. G. Jackson established Hockey on a permanent basis. E. A. G. Marlar was a splendid Rugby coach after the game was introduced, while from 1920 to his premature death, H. J. Butters was identified with the games, especially Hockey and Cricket. C. L. Harris took over the Rugby and for 21 years from the late thirties, F. M. Bancroft was in charge of Rugby and Cricket, to which games J. D. B. Milne also lent valuable assistance. In more recent years K. A. Davies, B. C. Richards, J. K. Brennan and B S. Duncan have taken and are taking on the responsibility of maintaining the old traditions. One of the features of the school has always been the variety of ways in which a boy could represent the school. Swimming and Athletics come readily to mind; for many years W. T. Lack was associated with Swimming, but it is only recently that Athletics have been treated seriously. Tennis, Fives, Golf, Badminton and Basketball are many other games which have from time to time attracted their adherents, while Chess and Table Tennis have a current vogue.

An early photograph of cricket on the playing field. The scorebox can be seen over by the trees. Note the sails on the mill, which were taken down in 1908, and the chimney alongside.

School Societies come and go in accordance with current trends, but there are some which are permanent. In 1923 a Scientific Society was formed. Its membership has been largely restricted (for obvious reasons) to the VIth form, and much valuably work has been done, and many places of industrial and scientific interest visited under the guidance of W. D. Coales, W. T. Lack and F. R. Speke.

From the school's early days there has been an interest in drama, though the original school builders made little provision for a stage, for lighting, or for the proper accommodation of an audience. W. F. Brown and Mrs. Thring were responsible for the early productions. Later G. Hart, who had some professional acting experience, took over. Performances took place on a platform constructed of boards on trestles, which creaked ominously at inconvenient moments. In 1920 A. C. Wadsworth took over, and very early in his Headmastership, A. F. R. Evans, himself a skilled carpenter, with the aid of L. A. Boskett created a wooden stage structure which could be erected when required for plays and afterwards taken down and stored. Footlights and over head lighting battens were contributed by W. T. Lack, draw curtains and flats were made, and by 1929 these improvements were in use. Further beneficial changes were made as funds permitted; the present stage structure and proscenium curtains were installed in 1954, much of the practical work being done by members of the VIth form. A School Fete, a grant from the Parents' Association and a contribution from the L. E. A. paid for these improvements, the Dramatic Society undertaking the refitting of the stage with curtains and lighting equipment. The work of the Dramatic Society has drawn together a large number of members of staff and boys in a co-operative and constructive effort, and over the years a particular debt has been owed to A. F. R. Evans, W. T. Lack, L. A. Boskett, R. H. Symes, F. R. Speke, T. H. Kidd, F. M. Bancroft, J. D. B. Milne. R. L. Poirier, and Dr. H. C. Ault. There have been a number of capable boy actors who have later made their mark in University societies and other acting spheres. J. Croall (known professionally as John Stewart) has been a popular stage and film actor for many years. Sam Kydd (a notable Maria in Twelfth Night) appears regularly on the television screen, while Godfrey Harrison, (Captain Absolute in the Rivals) is well known as the author of a "Life of Bliss". Shakespeare, Shaw, Sheridan, Goldsmith have been the authors chiefly featured. In recent years B. C. Arthur has taken over the work of production, and the society has just presented T. S. Eliot's "Murder in the Cathedral". During the past ten years performances of one act plays have also been given during the Easter term, by middle school and junior forms in addition to the Society itself, and these have provided a useful training ground for the more senior work.

The Glee Club has been mentioned elsewhere. There is now in existence a School Choir, begun by R. Warwick and continued by A. Hauke. The post of Music master was a part time one. Latterly W. B. Moore and R. L. Black have been appointed on a full time basis, and the School choir, apart from performing annually at the

Start of the Annual Steeplechase at Sewell, 1939

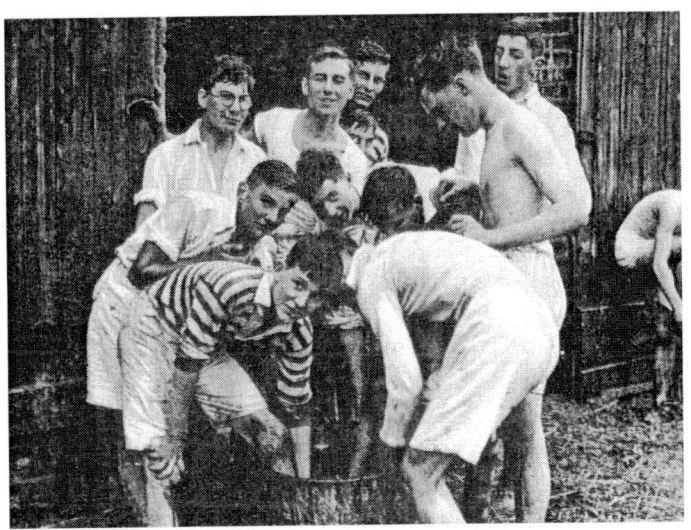

.... and the finish (washing and changing facilities!)

Duke of Edinburgh Award boys helping to make the film 'The Way Ahead'.

Young Robin Hoods at the School fete.

Priory Church on Founders Day and for the Carol Service, now contributes regular concerts and provides musical entertainment on Speech Dav.

An important development of recent years has been the establishment of the Duke of Edinburgh Award Scheme. When the Duke inaugurated the Pilot Scheme in 1956 we were invited to take part, and the original film of the scheme 'The Way Ahead' was partly made on the school premises and in Dunstable, displaying the activities of our own boys. The response to the challenge provided by the scheme has been most gratifying and the successes achieved bear comparison with those of any school or organisation in the country. Our boys have obtained 43 Gold Awards, 73 Silver Awards, and 130 Bronze Awards to date, and the training and discipline involved in the scheme may do something to repair the loss felt by the extinction of the Cadet Force. F. M. Bancroft has been in charge of the scheme from the time of its introduction: its especial value is that it first trains boys to discipline themselves voluntarily and then enables them to pass on their knowledge to others whether in school or in the wider world outside. Its benefits are available not merely to the brilliant athlete but to any average boy who has the courage and determination to strive to pass its various tests.

Under 15's Rugby team, 1968.

Chapter Ten

The Cadet Force

For 58 years of the school's life a notable feature was the existence of a flourishing Cadet Unit, beginning with the appointment in February 1903 of a Drill Instructor, and the formation, shortly afterwards, of the Cadet Corps. School Cadet units began in 1860, stemming from the volunteer Rifle Corps. These were purely local in character and were intended to provide a number of trained men for local defence in case of emergency. What began as a practical measure to contribute to national security became incorporated in the general school ethos, broadened its aims and became a training ground for leadership and good citizenship.

In 1903 every physically fit boy in the school, together with certain masters, undertook Company Drill in the Quadrangle, tactical drill in Dunstable Park, and physical drill every evening, Miniature Rifle Shooting was done in the Gymnasium (now the school library). In the following years shooting was done on an open (.303) range which then existed at Pascombe Pit on the Downs. In 1907 a blue serge uniform was introduced, but the Corps members disliked it and remained un-uniformed until the introduction in 1914 of a regulation khaki uniform. The Corps was then officially recognised in Army Orders and affiliated to the 5th Battalion, the Bedfordshire Regiment T.A. During the period 1914-18 the number of Cadet units increased and inter-unit competitions developed. Notable among these was the Lucas Tooth scheme for Physical Training, competitions being arranged annually in the counties. The School Corps won the Bedfordshire Trophy for several years consecutively, and when, after a lapse of some years, the competition was revived 1939-45, the School again won the trophy. The Corps also competed for the Imperial Challenge Shield Competition for Miniature Rifle Shooting within the Empire and Commonwealth. In 1919 a Drum & Bugle Band was initiated, and made such good progress that it played a prominent part in the Peace Day Celebrations in Dunstable, in July of that year.

From 1930-32 official recognition was for political reasons, withdrawn from Cadet units administered by County T.A. Associations. This led to the formation of a National Cadet Association, with the general administration of Cadet units in the hands of a County Committee. Badges and buttons bearing the School arms were adopted in place of those of the Beds. & Herts. Regiment, and when in 1932 affiliation to the regiment was resumed these were retained with the addition of the Regimental Collar Badges. Uniforms were supplied by private contract until 1942, since when they have been issued from Army sources.

A remarkable feature of the 1930s was the high standard of the band and the reputation it earned beyond its own locality. In the earlier days the Band had been

Cadet Corps Band, July 1931.

Cadet Corps Drum and Bugle Band - Cromwell Road, Luton, 1934.

helped by local musicians. In 1931, at the suggestion of R.S.M. Odell, several members on leaving school continued to attend, practices and to help with instruction. This led to the formation of an Old Boys section of the band, so that a really strong composite body could be turned out for ceremonial and other occasions. This efficiency and smartness brought many demands for their appearance at public functions, and their attendances included appearances at the Royal Berkshire Hospital Sunday parade, at Reading (1935—38) in which eight bands participated. The Old Boys' section by dances and other means raised money for instruments and equipment. A Band magazine was issued and a History of the Band published by the brothers Frank and John Dandy, who with B. W. B. Squires were indefatigable in their efforts to maintain and improve standards of performance.

The Old Boys' section was, of necessity, ended at the outbreak of the 1939-45 war: it left a very fine tradition. In 1944 a full set of Brass Band Instruments was acquired, and under Sgt. Major Murphy, who had trained at Kneller Hall, the band showed great enthusiasm, being especially encouraged by a visit from Sir Adrian Boult, who himself conducted them through some of their music. Regrettably, when the Local Authority took over the school it was found to have no power to continue the employment of the Corps instructor on the other School duties he had habitually performed, and so the services of Sgt. Major Murphy were lost, and the Brass Band section lapsed. The Corps band reverted to its former pattern and so remained for the rest of its life.

A keen interest was always taken in Miniature Rifle Shooting, with matches against other schools and competitions within the county. In 1930 and 1931 the school team won the Brine Cup at the Public Secondary Schools' Cadet Association Camp. B. W. B. Squires won a trophy for the highest individual score in Camp for three successive years. The whole Corps competed annually in the Imperial Challenge Shield Competition, being regularly placed in the selected Honours list. In 1940 the Corps won H. M. The King's Shield for the Cadet Unit achieving the highest score in the I.C.S. competition, and was placed 3rd in 1941 and 1942. In 1944 the Shooting Team was 1st of fourteen Bedfordshire schools competing in a National Competition, and 16th in the final results.

The Annual Camp was always a highlight, beginning in 1905 when L. C. R. Thring and Sgt. Major Odell took a party to Bisley. This was repeated in 1906, but attendance at camp was somewhat spasmodic owing to problems of catering for Territorials and schoolboys in the same camp. From 1927 the Corps regularly camped with the Public Secondary Schools Cadet Association, run by Schoolmaster officers. After 1948 the Services assumed responsibility for providing accommodation and training facilities in established camp sites on a vastly larger scale than hitherto.

The post war era brought a new look to pre-service training. Naval and Air Cadet units had come into being and all three Cadet branches in schools were in 1948 formed into a Combined Force, of which the School Corps became part, forming an additional Naval section. The services provided many courses in Technical Training, signalling, leadership, and so on, many of which were successfully attended by our boys. A significant development was a form of 'Arduous Training', in the performance of which mountaineering expeditions have been made to North Wales.

Sea Cadet Whaler Race - Luton Hoo, mid-1950s.

Cadet Corps, mid-1950s.

In 1960 the Centenary Celebrations of the Cadet Force were held. and on July 22nd two cadets represented the school at a Royal Parade at Buckingham Palace. Each school contributed a page to a Centenary Book presented to H. M. The Queen, the book being subsequently deposited at the Cadet Training Centre at Frimley Park. It was a matter for great regret that in 1961 it became clear that a decline in numbers affecting the maintenance grant of the C.C.F. made it impracticable to continue the unit, and it was quietly disbanded.

A list of Commanding Officers and Staff Instructors is appended, but it would be wrong to close this chapter without some reference to Lt. Col. A. C. Wadsworth whose services to the School unit and in a wider sphere were recognised by the award of the M.B.E. R.S.M. Odell, to whom tribute has been paid elsewhere, remains also in the memory as the finest type of man produced by the Army; his influence over several generations of boys was both wide and wise.

1903 School Volunteer Corps
1914 Dunstable School Cadet Corps
1941 "A" Company No. 1 Cadet Battalion
1945 Army Cadet Force
1948 Combined Cadet Force

Commanding Officers

Capt. H. J. Butters -	1918
Capt. A. R. Thompson	1921
Capt. E. A. G. Marlar -	1927
Maj. A. C. Wadsworth	1929
Capt. W. N. Brook -	1941
Lt. Col. A. C. Wadsworth, M.B.E.	1948
Capt. R. F. Broadfoot -	1949

Staff Instructors

Sgt. Odell -	1903-14
Sgt. Clark -	1914
C. S. M. Diggle	1914-19
R. S. M. Odell	1919-36
Sgt. Danton	1936-37
Sgt. Jackson	1987-39
R. S. M. Meal	1940-41
R. S. M. Murphy -	1944-48

These details are as represented on the page in the Cadet Unit Book presented to Her Majesty.

CHAPTER ELEVEN

The Old Dunstablians' Club

As soon as a sufficient number of boys had passed through the school to make the project worthwhile an Old Dunstablians' Club was formed. It was certainly in existence by 1899. Complete details of the organisation and officials of those early days were lost when the minute books disappeared towards the end of the first World War, but some information has come down through the early magazines and from the older Old Boys. A leading figure in the formation of the club was J. T. Phillipson, and the earliest Club secretary appears to have been G. O. Anderson, who had a long and active association with the school and Club. Certainly the first Annual Dinner was held before 1899. For many years these dinners took place in London, the earliest at the Holborn Restaurant. In the years prior to 1914 a considerable number of boys came from the London area while many Old Boys travelled to London daily on business, which perhaps suggests a reason for dining in London. Certainly for many years a variety of venues in London were meeting places for Old Boys, notably the "Ship" in Whitehall, where a regular monthly gathering took place until the 1930s. The first Old Dunstablians' Cricket week was arranged for 1900, and this annual gathering continued, war years excepted, until 1930. F. H. Webb gathered together many sides in those days, and after the war J. A. Webdale was the organiser. Regular opponents appear to have been the Old Bedford Modernians and the Old Finchleians, and regular players at one time or another were, L. C. R. Thring, W. F. Brown, T. Brown, E. E. Apthorp, J. B. Escolme, F. H. Webb, H. J. Butters, H. W. Seaman, A. F. Waller and J. A. Webdale. One of the early ventures of the Old Boys was the running of the Magazine. Because so few copies were sold the magazine was always in difficulties: in its early days there was, of course, little general news, but the decision of the Old Boys to take charge of it brought a decline in school news to balance an increase of Old Boys news, and the venture was abandoned. From time to time shooting and swimming matches took place against the school. One of the shooting stalwarts of those early days was F. A. Austin, who gave a cup to the corps for annual competition and who was a regular figure at Bisley. Many of a later generation will remember Fred as a loyal servant of the O. D. Club, and few will quickly forget his stirring rendering of "Kissing Cup" at the dinners.

On the retirement of L. C. R. Thring in 1921 the Old Boys organised a Cricket Festival. This was in the hands of J. A. Webdale, for many years the Sports Secretary to the Club, and following this A. E. Thomson was given the task of bringing together the Club once more. By 1922 it had been re-formed, with W. F. Brown as President, and C. Hyder as Secretary. Occasional dinners were still to be

Old Boys Cricket Match - any summer term.

Part of the Old Score Box - are your initials here?

held in London, but gradually they were moved to Luton and of recent years they have taken place at Dunstable. Throughout its life the club has lacked a permanent local headquarters, and all attempts to purchase a ground sufficient for the full needs of the members have failed; the Hockey and the Rugby sections have therefore been compelled to make their own arrangements. A cricket section has functioned at various times, notably during the 1939-45 war, but the lack of a ground has proved fatal to its continued existence. In recent years C. M. Butler has organised an annual Golf match against the Old Lutonians; the last match featured 22 players on each side, and it is hoped the numbers may increase. The traditional O.D. Matches with the school are the Rugby, Hockey and Cricket games at the end of each term. From time to time there have been Swimming, Tennis and Shooting matches, and this year a Badminton match was arranged. Among the Old Boys who, apart from those mentioned elsewhere, have in recent years made a public reputation are Sir Charles Lockhart, a distinguished Colonial administrator, N. F. Morris, Professor of Gynaecology at Charing Cross Hospital and a pioneer of new medical techniques; A. C. Spearing, a don at Cambridge, Michael Barrett, winning recognition as an author and film script writer; R. A. Gibbs, Governing Director of Home Counties Newspapers, and his Brother J. Gibbs, also a Director; R. C. W. Dinsdale, Consultant Dental surgeon at Sheffield United Hospitals and Lecturer in Oral Pathology at Sheffield University, G. Colson, who captained the Oxford University R. F. C. Many Old Boys have served as members of the Board of Governors. C. Hyder was at one time Chairman, a position now held by R. W. S. Smith. J. W. L. French is the club representative on the Board, while P. N. Wainwright and R. Summerson are other Governors with long club associations. The club presents prizes annually for Arts & Science subjects, and is responsible for purchasing the portraits of former Headmasters and long serving members of staff for the School Hall. It has also now accepted from the original Memorial Committee the task of administrating the War Memorial Fund.

The Hockey Club

In 1925 under the auspices of the present club a Hockey section was formed. A.F. Waller, supported by C. Hyder, C. R. Blinco, T. R. Worthington and J. Beasley were the pioneers; the first captain was F. Taylor. No ground was available so that the early years were difficult and travelling expenses were heavy, yet the club survived, and in 1936 prospects improved. A ground was obtained from Messrs Bagshawe at Dunstable and two teams were regularly fielded. With the outbreak of the war the club disbanded, those players who remained joining with members of the Luton Town H. C. to form the Remnants. The club was re-formed for the 1946-47 season and played on the Kingsway Recreation Ground, Luton. By 1951-52 three teams regularly represented the club, and by degrees it became possible to obtain the use of Wardown Park, the present headquarters. In 1961-2 a fourth XI was formed. The first foreign trip was undertaken to Germany in 1938, and a visit was made to Belgium in 1939. Before the war Easter tours were made to the Clacton Festival; in more recent years many numbers have played at the Folkestone Festival for the Bedfordshire Eagles, and now the club contributes 90 per cent of the Eagles' players. In 1946 the club won the Vauxhall six-a-side tournament, under the captaining of 'Mumpy' Warren, and has once reached the final since. Many of its players have represented Bedfordshire, while others have played for Hertfordshire and Surrey. D. R. P. Blake and P. C. Webb have played for the Eastern Counties.

The Rugby Club

In 1927 a Rugby section was formed. A ground was obtained at Fensome's field in Leagrave, where a familiar sight at lunchtime on a winter Saturday was that of R. B. Waller, C. Pedder and C. M. Butler clearing the field for an afternoon match. Unfortunately there were never enough regular players, and after struggling along for three seasons the section was forced to disband. Most of the players joined Luton R.F.C., while R. B. Waller became a pillar of the Hockey Club.

In 1947 a new start was made by a small group including B. J. Reason, J. Baker, G. Sandifer, J. Hamilton, F. P. Rowe, and F. M. Bancroft. A. G. S. Reed was the first captain, with B. J. Reason secretary and G. Sandifer treasurer. Everyone worked with a will to raise funds. A ground was secured near French's Avenue and later off Luton Rd., but a great step forward was made in 1954 when a ground was leased in Bull Pond Lane, the opening of which was marked by a visit from an East Midlands XV. A. E. D. Eyles and J. W. L. French were now associated with the club; their continuing interest has proved invaluable, as has the support of Rugby lovers such as D. Edgley, W. J. Morgan, G. Combes, and J. Power. Shortly afterwards a pavilion was erected and in 1961, with the help of the Rugby Union, it became possible to purchase the ground. Membership of the club has steadily increased, and now five teams are turned out each week. A recent achievement of the club has been the winning in April of this year of the Chiltern seven-a-side tournament.

The Old Dunstablians' Lodge

A number of Old Boys considered the formation of a School Lodge in the years preceding 1939, but the project had to be postponed because of the outbreak of the war. Eventually it was found possible to proceed with the plan, and the Lodge was consecrated in the School Hall on September 9th, 1944. A feature of the consecration was the address given by the Rev. Joseph Moffett, O.B.E., D.D., Past Grand Master of Hertfordshire .

The Lodge has been fortunate in having the use of the School premises for its meetings, and the ties of memory and association have proved to be strong. The Founders of the Lodge thought that members might be brought in from a distance, but in recent years the Boarding House catered largely for the needs of boys in the Home Counties, which has resulted in the Lodge having rather a local character. As the School has become purely a day school this characteristic will necessarily persist.

The first Worshipful Master of the Lodge was the late W.Bro. A. N. Gutteridge, P.C.Std.Br., P.Pr.G.W., while another Grand Officer W.Bro. G. C. C. Hinton, P.G.Std.Br., P.Pr.G.W. has also been a tower of strength. The Lodge has been particularly fortunate in enjoying the services of W.Bro. R. W. S. Smith, P.Pr.G.W., who, with one short interval, has served as Secretary since the consecration.

The Lodge is a member of the Federation of School Lodges and acted as host to the Federation's Annual Festival in 1959.

PRESIDENTS OF O.DS'. CLUB

1920-1	L. C. R. Thring	1950	A. F. Waller
1922-3	W. F. Brown	1951	G. H. Bailey
1924-5	E. E. Apthorp	1952	C. M. Butler
1926-7	A. E. Thomson	1953	R. Summerson
1928-9	C. H. Dixon	1954	F. M. Bancroft
1930-1	A. F. R. Evans	1956	J. Mayne
1932-3	J. E. Briggs	1956	A. D. Philpot
1934-5	C. Hyder	1957	T. R. Worthington
1936	F. A. Austin	1958	C. O. Bishop
1937	J. L. Mallett	1959	J. W. L. French
1938	G. O. Anderson	1960	D. R. P. Blake
1939	J. A. Webdale	1961	F. Cadle
1940	B. H. Gray	1962	D. T. Jarvis
1941	R. B. Waller	1963	S. W. P. Blake
1942	C. L. Harris	1964	K. W. Brown
1943	H. J. Butters	1965	A. E. D.Eyles
1944	W. D. Coales	1966	A. S. Bennett
1945	C. H. Le May	1967	C. P. H.Williams
1946	R. W. S. Smith	1968	S. Summerson
1947	L. A. Boskett	1969	E. G. Baldock
1948	P. N. Wainwright	1970	P. K. E. Ball
1949	H. S. Mower	1971	W. T. Lack

PRESIDENTS OF HOCKEY CLUB

A R. Thompson, A. F. R. Evans, H. J. Butters, R. B. Waller, C. W. L. Warren.

PRESIDENTS OF RUGBY CLUB

G. H. Bailey, F. M. Bancroft, J. D. B. Milne, A. E. D. Eyles,
J. W. L. French, J. A. Hamilton.

Members of Staff

HEADMASTERS

L. C. R. Thring J.P., M.A.	1888 — 1921
A. R. Thompson M.A.	1921 — 1927
A. F. R. Evans J.P., M.A.	1927 — 1948
G. H. Bailey M.A.	1948 — 1960
L. P. Banfield M. A..	1960 — 1971

E. S. Allen	1911 — 1913
W. Allen B.A.	1962 — 1965
E. E. Apthorp B.A.	1900 —1915, 1918 —1929
	Second Master
B. C. Arthur M.A.	1959 — 1966
H. C. Ault M.A., D.Litt.	1948 — 1959
W. F. Ball*	1948 — 1949
A. H. Baker B.A.	1961
F. M. Bancroft M.A.	1934 — 1970
C. Barry* A.R.C.A.	1937 — 1940
E. H. Bates B.A.	1961 — 1966
A. R. Baxter B.A.	1961 — 1969
L. O. Beater M.A.	1908
R. Bedford*	1956 — 1957
B. B. Belcher B.Sc.	1919 — 1920
W. W. Benert M.A.	1954 — 1956
R. L. Black G.R.S.M.	1960 — 1965
W. Booth M.A.	1916 — 1917
L. A. Boskett B.Sc.	1920 — 1959
J. A. Brennan D.L.C.	1955 — 1971
J. E. Briggs	1908 — 1909
W. O. Brigstocke B.A.	1923 — 1925
R. F. Broadfoot B.A.	1947 — 1971
W. N. Brock B.A.	1929 — 1960
W. F. Brown	1894 — 1924
	Second Master
F. W. O. Buckhold Ph.D.	1920 — 1923
H. J. Butters	1918 — 1950
F. Cadle B.A.	1930 — 1961
L. CernyB.A	1958 — ?
F. B. Chapman Ph.D.	1959 — 1961
? Clarke	1889 ?
W. D. Coales B.Sc.	1909 — 1919, 1921 — 1959
	Second Master
J. O. J. Cowgill	1921
A. W. Creswell	1913 — 1914

* — Part Time member of staff.

K. A. Davies D.L.C.	1954 — 1961
P. S. Davies*	1950 — 1951
Col. Davson	1947
H. C. Deacon*	1916 — 1922
H. R. Dean B.Sc.	1924
D. W. Dearne B.Sc.	1959 — 1960
D. H. Drysdale B.A.	1958 — 1960
B. S. Duncan B.Sc.	1961 — ?
C. Edwards	1921 — 1923
F. S. J. Eldridge B.A.	1943 — 1945
J. B. Escolme B.A.	1904 — 1910
R .A. Evans B.A.	1960 — 1962
? Evans	? — 1908
A. F. Forster	1958 — 1962
A. E. Fraser*	1950
T. Fritschi	1914 — 1920
P. J. Frogley B.A.	1957 — 1960
? Gaskell	? — 1904
G. R. Gibbs B.A.	1961 — ?
T. H. Ginn B.A.	1960 — 1962
F. Gostelow*	1890 — 1916
C. H. E. Govier B. A .	1927 — 1929
S. J. Gray*	1952 — 1955
T. E. Green B.Sc.	1915 — 1919
H . H . M . Hall	1920
P. A. W. Harrington B.A.	1962 — 1964
C. L. Harris	1923 — 1944
G. L. Hart	1917 — 1929
P. Haswell B.A.	1910 — 1911
M. J. Hateley B.A.	1961 — 1964
A. Hauke G.R.S.M.	1954 — 1956
J. Healing	1888
S. J. Heddon	1911
G. W. Hedges*	1922 — ?
C. Heldman	1913 — 1915
D. W. Hendra B.Sc	1962 — 1964
A. Hillier*	1911 — 1913
J. V. Horwood B.A.	1951 — 1961
W. E. G. Jackson B.A.	1908 — 1911
G. W. A. Jenner B.A.	1962 — ?
J. T. Johnson* M.A.	1918 — 1919
F. A. Jones B.A.	1908 — 1909

* — Part Time member of staff.

? Kaye	1904 — 1906
R. Keable M.A.	1921 — 1922
J. H. Kenamis B.A.	1906
T. H. Kidd B.A.	1920 — 1934
H. J. W. Kingston	1909 — 1911
W. J. Kissick B.A.	1961 — 1962 *(Exchange)*
W. F. Knight B.A.	1911 — 1915
W. T. Lack O.B.E., J.P. B.Sc.	1924 —1965
	Deputy Headmaster
P. D. Lawman B.A.	1962 — 1967
J. E. G. Leech R.Sc	1908 — 1909
C. Y. Le Huray B.A,	1921 — 1943
? Macassey	1906
H. A. V. Macfarlane M.A.	1934 — 1936
R. L. Mackie M.A.	1909 — 1911
E. A. G. Marlar B.A.,L.L.B.	1923 — 1928
F. Martin B.A.	1910 — 1913
J. G. Matthewman B.A,	1944 — 1971
G. NcNish	1960 — 1961 *(Exchange)*
J, L. Meigh B.A.	1951 — 1953
J. D. B. Milne B.A.	1944 — 1967
D. W. Mollison B.Sc.	1959
P. S. Moondi B.Sc.	1962
W. B. Moore B.Mus.	1956 — 1960
J. G. Morris B.A.	1962 — 1965
G. H. Morse - Boycott	1918 — 1919
L. Muggeridge B.D.	1962 — 1963
J. D. Munro M.A.	1961
? Newman	? — 1904
A. C. M. Orrey	1906 — 1908
W. Otter*	1913 — 1919
T. C. Pacey*	1943 — 1948
G. V. Pagden B.A.	1942 — 1943
A . E. Pank	1962
J. Parry B.A.	1929
J. J. Parsons B.A.	1950 — 1951
A. A. J. Pennycook B.A.	1959 — 1961
J. T. Phillipson M.A.	1890 — 1894
	Second Master
D. R. Pike B.A.	1960 — 1961
R. L. Poirier B.Lettres	1929 — 1943
? Price	1917 — 1918

* — Part Time member of staff.

B. C. Richards B.A.	1956 — 1960
J. A. V. Richards B.A.	1943
W. Ridge B.A.	1923
R. Rigby M.A.	1944 — 1947
W. H. Rose D.L.C.	1949 — 19S0
A. E. Ruthven-Murray B.A.	1920 — 1921
E. R. Scholes*	1948 — 1951
A. C. Schwab M.A.	1940
C. H. Scott M.A.,B.D.	1944 — 1950
T. A. C. Sharp	1909 — 1910
B. W. Simpson B.Sc.	1959 — 1964
? Smith B.A.	1904 — 1906
H. W. L. Smith*	1945 — 1948
F. R. Speke M.A.	1936 — 1971
Rev. H. Staunton	1890 — ?
E. L. Sturges B.A.	1919 — 1921
R. B. Swift M.A.	1961 — 1962
R. H. Symes B.Sc	1941 — 1971
A. H. Taylor M.A.	1911 — 1913
W. C . Thorley	1915
J. Thorne*	1920 — 1943
G. F. Todd D.L.C.	1962 — 1963
A. C. Towell D.L.C.	1950 — 1954
S. R. Unwin B.A.	1941 — 1942
E. R. Venables B.A.	1943 — 1944
P. Wade B.A.	1958
A. C. Wadsworth M.B.E.,M.A.	1929 — 1962
R. Warwick G.C.S.M.	1950 — 1953
H. H. Whincop B.A.	1916
W. R. Wilkinson B.A.	1915
H. V. Williams*	1909 — 1912
R. Windross B.A.	1925 — 1926
C. J. Wood B.Sc.	1961 — ?
J. C. Wood B.Sc.	1955 — ?
B. H. Yemm B.A.	1956 — 1964
A. Ziegler* A.R.C.A.	1940 — 1943

* — Part Time member of staff.

Miss L. Allingham	1916 — 1919
Miss O. G. Avent	1917 — 1919
Miss P. M. S. Benning	1913
Miss L. R. Clarke	1919
Miss M. Draper*	1920 — 1937
Miss M. M. Lawson	1919 — 1921
Miss M. N. Moody*	1909 — 1915
Miss A. E. Morgan	1920
Miss G. E. Ranger*	1912 — 1920
Mrs. D. Taylor A.R.C.A.	1943 — ?
Miss C. E. Waller*	1890
Miss D. G. Wilkes	1914 — 1916

* —Part Time member of staff.

ADDITIONAL AND REPLACEMENT
MEMBERS OF STAFF 1964 - 1971

L.I.ADAM-HILL	1965-1969
E.BADEVILLE	1964-1971
D.BEXON	1966-1971
R.J.CHAPMAN	1968-1971
B.CIRCUIT	1965-1971
W.P.DAVIES	1965-1971
P.DIXON	1967-1971
W.FREWIN	1964-1971
P.GILL	1967-1971
A.GOODWIN	1964-1967
T.H.F.GRAY	1965-1968
B.GUIRAND	1969-1971
R.D.HOBSON	1968-1971
G.HOPKINS	1966-1967
R.W.LANCASTER	1967-1969, 1970-1971
M.D.LAWS	1968-1971
K.LUMMA	1968-1971
C.MARTEN	1969-1971
P.A.MASON	1968-1971
C.D.MARFITT-SMITH	1969-1970
G.McCANN	1969-1971
H.McMULLEN	1964-1971
P.J.MITCHELL	1967-1971
R.MOORE	1966-1971
A.OLLIVIER	1968-1971
E.PARRY	1965-1968
A.F.PEMBLETON	1965-1966
J.M.REMINGTON	1964-1969
B.K.RIGBY	1964-1971
M.G.SEATH	1968-1971
R.STOCK	1967-1971
J.L.WALKER	1967-1971
R.S.WALKER	1964-1967
M.I.J.WOODWARD	1964-1971
F.E.WYBURGH	1967-1968
FRAULEIN KOENIG	1965-1966
MLLE.M.C.MARIN	1965-1966
MISS M. SUTCLIFFE	1969
MISS P.A.TABERNACLE	1964-1965
MRS WOODWARD	1969-1971

Hankey Gold Medal

Thomson Hankey Esq., first Chairman of the Governors, bequeathed a sum of money the income from which was to provide an annual award for the boy who had made the best use of his opportunities during his life at school. The list of winners of the award to date appears below.

1890	W. Gray	1929	J. F. Saunders
1891	O. G. Anderson	1930	D. McK. Moore
1892	E. Spencer	1931	R. M. Vance
1893	F.E.F. Cobley, H.C. Cripps		
1894	R. E. Hornby	1932	E. H. Clarke
1895	G. A. Marsh	1933	E. J. Dunford
1896	R. A. Gladwell		
1897	J. Parkin	1934	R. Tompkins
1898	K. Heighway	1935	K. J. Nott
1899	C. S. Benning	1936	D. R. P. Blake
1900	E. V. Watkins	1937	P. A. Waller
1901	A. O. F. Cobley	1938	N. F. Morris
1902	E. N. Bewley	1939	H. R. Oakley
1903	R. H. Waller	1940	S. W. P. Blake
1904	C. D. K. Seaver	1941	G. A. Duncan
1905	P. Haswell	1942	I. K. Bennett
1906	J. E. Briggs	1943	A. J. S. Harrison
1907	J. G. Wylde	1944	R. C. W. Dinsdale
1908	R. P. Ellis	1945	A. J. Alabastes
1909	R. L. Klosz	1946	J. A. Fendley
1910	R. G. Gutteridge	1947	B. J. Reason
1911	K. S. Roden	1948	B. Butters
1912	J. W. Westwood	1949	J. A. Akroyd
1913	N. B. Green	1950	R. G. Knowles
1914	S. A. Stimpson	1951	F. W. Bullock
1915	A. E. Thring	1952	J. H. Bell
1916	H. W. Seaman	1953	J. Forsdyke
1917	C. O. S. B. Brooke	1954	M. J. Selby
1918	F. D. Williamson	1955	G. T. Iggleden
1919	W. R. Healing	1956	R. G. H. Record
1920	T. C. Hewson	1957	P. Mc Arthur
1921	F. R. Brown	1958	P. G. Baldock
1922	R. G. Streeton	1959	L. J. Moore
1923	W. F. B. Lovett	1960	J. R. Thorogood
1924	A. L. Butt	1961	G. W. Mountjoy
1925	H. J. Squires	1962	A. Brown
1926	R. F. P. Morris	1963	J. Hodgson
1927	H. F. Hunt	1964	A. B. W. Flowerdew
1928	F. A. Cassidy	1965	D. Taylor

In Memoriam

When I am dead, think only this of me
that there's some corner of a foreign field that is for ever England.
Rupert Brooke

1899— 1901

H. Anderson   J. Anderson

1914—1918

E. C. Bailey
C. Banks
M. S. Benning
E. Bewley
W. H. Brantom
W. Brown
C. F. Burley
S. Burnett
R. Chatterton
D. Cockerell
E. F. Collins
B. S. Cumberland
B. P. Cuxson
P. Darby
R. Deacon
H. E. Dewar
M. W. Dickens
H. B. Gordon
R. B. W. Gosse
E. A. Grace
R. Green
R. C. Gutteridge
G. Hahn
K. Healing
G. H. H. Henderson
W. Hesseltine
A. W. Hopkins
V. Jepson
C. Jones
F. A. Key
R. D. King

W. F. Knight
J. Longridge
J. S. Leese
A. Lewis
A. Lockhart
R. Looker
O. T. Millard
E. R. P. Muddock
H. Muddock
J. M. P. Muddock
R. Nevill
C. Oliver
W. H. Ostler
W. F. Paddock
V. H. Playfair
G. L. Reid
A. Rose
J. Sansom
T. Shervington
W. Shervington
G. Schunck
J. H. S. Simons
E. Squires
S. Stimson
R. S. Strange
T. W. Stubley
P. Thomson
A. E. Thring
L. Warren
J. P. Waters
J. W. Westwood
B. T. Wilkins

1939—1945

A J. Bezant
K. S. Bird
K. L. O. Blow
D. M. A. Brown
F. T. Buckingham
D. T. Butcher
P. C. Chappell
R. A. Chignell
D. Clark
R. I. Cosson
H. V. Day
R. A. H. Dolan
E. G. Francis
R. Freak
T. J. Goodwin
C. C. Gurney
C. B. Harrison
A. H. Hayward
J. A. Horn
G. Irons
K. F. Jeffs
P. J. Jeffs
S. G. Keast

R. F. Kelly
G. R. Knight
R. Leno
R. H. Oakley
F. Overell
C. J. Palmer
K. G. Parker
A. R. Potter
E. C. Raddon
P H. Richards
W. P. Richards
D. C. Richardson
C. J. Rudd
L. F. Squire
B. W. B. Squires
F. S. Thripp
D G. Tompkins
F G. Underwood
A. G. Wainwright
R. Warren
L. B. P. White
J. G. Wylde

Decorations

1914— 1918

C.B.	Paymaster-Commander E. W. C. Thring, R.N.
V.C.	Col. E. E. D. Henderson
D.S.O.	Commander C. S. Benning
D.S.C.	Lieut.-Commander G. A. C. Sharp, R.N.
	Surgeon J. Kelly, R.N.
M.C.	Lieut. H. E. Dewar (recommended for V.C.)
	Capt. K. Douglas
	Lt. Col. P. G. Douglas
	Capt. N. Elgood
	Major L. D. Henderson (and Bar)
	Capt. F. A, M. B. Jenkins
	Lieut. R. Nevill
	Lieut. C. Samm
	Lieut. C. E. Turner
	Lieut. F. S. Tooley (and mentioned in despatches)
D.C.M.	2nd Lieut. W. H. Brantom
M.M.	C.S.M. G. Harmer
	2nd Lieut. A. E. Pitcher
	M. Lockhart, R.A.M.C.

Royal Humane Society's Medal.

Midshipman F. C.N.G. Thursby

Foreign Decorations

ITALIAN	Paymaster-Commander E. W C. Thring, R.N. *Order of St. Maurice & St. Lazarus.*
FRENCH	Capt. F. M. Hughes *Croix de Chevalier, Legion d'honneur.* Bernard Billingham *Croix de Chevalier, Legion d'honneur. (awarded 1998)*
	Lieut. C. E. Turner, *Croix de Guerre*
	D. Peters, *Croix de Guerre*
	M. Lockhart, *Croix de Guerre*
RUSSIAN	Lt.-Commander G. A. C. Sharpe R.N. *Order of St. George, Order of St. Vladimir.*

1939—1945

Knighthood	Charles Lockhart
D.S.O.	Maj. General F. A. M. B. Jenkins, O.B.E., M.C.
D.F.C.	F/Lt. J. S. Adams
	W/O K. Blow
	F/O A. E. D. Eyles
	F/Lt. J. W. L. French
	F/O C. L. Hughes
	F/O K. J. Nott
M.C.	Lieut. R. N. Gutteridge
	Major C. J. Rudd (and Bar)
O.B.E.	C. E. Staddon
	F/Lt. R. B. Waller
M.B.E.	Capt. J. D. Blake
	E. F. Nott
Mentioned in Despatches	Major J. L. Mallett
	F/Lt. R. B. Waller

Foreign Award

NORWEGIAN War Medal	Lt. J. C. Hafner, R.N.V.R.

Cyprus, 1959

G.M.	Sgt. A. T. Taylor

86

Advice to all leaving school.

Give thy thoughts no tongue,
Nor any unproportion'd thought his act.
Be thou familiar, but by no means vulgar.
Those friends thou hast, and their adoption tried,
Grapple them to thy soul with hoops of steel;
But do not dull thy palm with entertainment
Of each new-hatch' d, unfledged comrade .
Beware of entrance to a quarrel, but being in,
Bear't that the opposed may beware of thee.
Give every man thy ear, but few thy voice;
Take each man's censure, but reserve thy judgment.
Costly thy habit as thy purse can buy,
But not express'd in fancy; rich, not gaudy;
For the apparel oft proclaims the man.
Neither a borrower nor a lender be;
For loan oft loses both itself and friend,
And borrowing dulls the edge of husbandry.
This above all: to thine ownself be true,
And it must follow, as the night the day,
Thou canst not then be false to any man.

William Shakespeare (1564—1616)

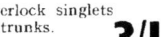

IT was in 1840, when Luton was a country town without a railway, and the motor car had never been dreamed of, that the business which was to become Gibbs and Dandy, Ltd., was first established.

The people who founded it were named neither Gibbs nor Dandy —but were, in fact, none other than Frederick Brown and Joseph Green, founders of the firm of Brown and Green, Ltd., which is still in existence in Luton today.

Their ironmongery business was established in a yard on Market Hill, and was evidently a successful venture. For in 1842 they came out of the obscurity of that yard and took the premises in George Street.

In 1844, they decided to become manufacturers as well as merchants, and established Luton's first ironfoundry.

It was, in effect, that decision by Messrs. Brown and Green that led to the name of Gibbs and Dandy, Ltd., being one of the best known in Luton's business life today. For the ironmongery side of the business in George Street was sold to Mr. C. F. Gibbs.

When Mr. Gibbs sold out in 1894 it was to two brothers, Mr. William Dandy and Mr. Percy Dandy, who had come to Luton from Peterborough. He left the business completely—so, although the firm has become famous as Gibbs and Dandy, there never was, in fact, a Gibbs and a Dandy in the business at the same time. The name of Gibbs was retained because it already had a tremendous goodwill value. Mr. William and Mr. Percy Dandy carried on the business as a partnership until 1920, when a private limited company was formed, and all the time the firm continued to register a steady growth.

During all these years, the firm had been expanding its premises, as well as extending the range of goods in which it dealt, to cope with the growing needs of a district which was becoming more and more industrialised, and was rapidly increasing in population. As far back as 1910. the first Dunstable branch was opened at 6 Church Street, and in 1923 these premises were extended by the acquisition of the adjoining shop. Other premises were added more recently.

Today, the firm's property extends over four acres, and the number of employees exceeds 250.

Firms and other enterprises with regular accounts include builders, plumbers, painters and decorators, carpenters and joiners, electricians, electrical engineers, architects and surveyors, and estate agents. Then there are the nationalised industries, County and Borough Councils, Hospital Groups, schools, engineers, engineering works, motor car and aircraft manufacturers, foundries, garages, timber merchants, farmers, farriers, coachbuilders, breweries, hotels, caterers and shop keepers. In fact, there is scarcely an enterprise in the district, large or small, that doesn't use some commodity stocked by

GIBBS AND DANDY, LIMITED
Builders' Merchants and Ironmongers
LUTON AND DUNSTABLE

Sincere Congratulations

on this

Anniversary

from the

Official Outfitters

65 George Street & 6 King Street
LUTON

Important   notice
for the attention
of members of the
Old Dunstablians Club

●

Your O.D. Ties, Scarves
a n d   Blazer   Badges
can be obtained from

●

E. J. Buckle and Son.

24 High Street South
DUNSTABLE

and

L. G. French (Outfitters) Ltd.

48 New Bedford Road
(C o r n e r   o f   M i l l   S t r e e t)
LUTON

Robinson & White Ltd.

BUILDING CONTRACTORS

Edward Street Dunstable

Telephone: Dunstable 61183

•

•

BUILDING SITES
available
throughout
the district
f o r
**RESIDENTIAL
DEVELOPMENT**

OTHER DUNSTABLE TITLES, 2002.

EXPLORING HISTORY ALL AROUND
Vivienne Evans

**Exploring History
All Around**

A handbook of local history, arranged as a series of routes to cover Bedfordshire and adjoining parts of Hertfordshire and Buckinghamshire. It is organised as two books in one. There are seven thematic sections full of fascinating historical detail and anecdotes for armchair reading. Also it is a perfect source of family days out as the book is organised as circular motoring/cycling explorations, highlighting attractions and landmarks. Also included is a background history to all the major towns in the area, plus dozens of villages, which will enhance your appreciation and understanding of the history that is all around you!

Vivienne Evans

DUNSTAPLE:
A TALE OF THE WATLING HIGHWAY
The legend of Dunne the Robber
A.W. Mooring

Dunstaple...a dramatic historical romance, which will particularly fascinate anyone interested in the legends of Dunstable's past. The story is woven around the tale of Dunne the Robber, the man whose exploits were said by some to be the basis for the town's modern name.

A.W. Mooring, editor of The Dunstable Borough Gazette between 1895 and 1909, took the gist of the legend about the outlaws who infested the forests around Dunstable crossroads in the time of King Henry 1, and added a romantic tale set among the Totternhoe caverns and the ramparts of Maiden Bower.

It first appeared as a six-month serial in The Gazette in 1898 and the following year in two different hardback editions produced in the newspaper's printing works in Albion Street, Dunstable.

PROUD HERITAGE
A brief history of Dunstable 1000-2000AD
Vivienne Evans

Dunstable was founded by a king, had a palace, a very important Augustian Priory and until 1600 was visited by nearly every king and queen of England. Sited on the crossroads less than forty miles from London. Oxford and Cambridge, Dunstable has been involved in many national events. Its populace has had to face economic and religious upheavals, but time after time Dunstablians pulled together, changed direction and won through to another successful era. Devoting a chapter to each of the ten centuries of the millennium, this book first sets the national and county scene in order to make more comprehensible the purely Dunstable events. Included in this book are stories about the Priory Church, Priory House, Kingsbury, Grove House, the Sugar Loaf and other inns, Ashton St Peter and other schools, Middle Row, Edward Street and other roads, the straw hat industry and the growth of the town.

DUNSTABLE WITH THE PRIORY 1100-1550
Vivienne Evans

This is the dramatic story of Henry I's busy and influential town with its royal palace, Augustinian Priory, Dominican Friary and thriving businesses around a major crossroads. Its rapid rise to success sees it linked to many famous national issues such as Magna Carta, the Eleanor Crosses, the Peasants' Revolt, the annulment of Henry VIII's marriage and the dissolution of the monasteries.

DUNSTABLE IN TRANSITION 1550-1700
Vivienne Evans

The residents of Dunstable needed all their resourcefulness to rebuild the town's success without the Augustinian Priory. Though disrupted by civil war, the developing coaching industry soon filled Dunstable with inns, as some new visitors brought wealth and importance to counterbalance other travellers who posed problems of poverty and disease. The age's religious upheavals found a microcosm in Dunstable. The majority stayed worshipping at the Priory Church, but some left for America and others met in secret until reform led to the acceptance of Quakers and Baptists. Scandal punctuated this period of turmoil - the baptism of a sheep at church, the hounding of a suspected witch and the predations of notorious highwaymen. All elements of Dunstable in a volatile, transitional phase.

HISTORIC INNS OF DUNSTABLE
Vivienne Evans

A fascinating booklet including an introductory essay covering the chronological histories of the entire town centre inns, over fifty in total. As well as special double page features on the ten most historically interesting buildings, the publication is well illustrated and includes a useful map of the locations.

DUNSTABLE DOWN THE AGES
An outline history from prehistoric to modern times
Joan Schneider & Vivienne Evans

People have lived in South Bedfordshire for thousands of years, even before the Romans constructed Watling Street, and a town grew up where Dunstable now stands on the crossing with the Icknield Way. Then came Anglo-Saxon imigrants, and the creation of a new town and a Priory by Henry I. There was a royal residence, and a Queen Eleanor cross was built after her coffin rested at the Priory. The decision, which ended Henry VIII's first marriage and caused England's break with the Roman Catholic Church, was taken here. Almshouses and schools were founded on the proceeds of distilling gin. Long distance coaches appeared on improved roads, and inns for travellers, but there were highwaymen too. Straw bonnets sold to travellers started the hat trade, which flourished in Victorian times. All these aspects are covered in this valuable publication, written as an introduction for all ages. Illustrated with dozens of line drawings.

DUNNO'S ORIGINALS
The First Complete Edition

A facsimile of five booklets concerning the history of Dunstable and its vicinity, including Totternhoe, Eaton Bray, Toddington, Flitwick and Flitton, first published in 1821 and 1822. Also four similar, rediscovered, and newly set manuscripts, completed by the author in 1823 shortly before his death, but previously unpublished. New introduction and glossary by John Buckledee, editor of the Dunstable Gazette.

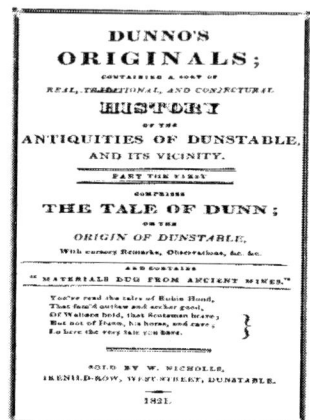

25 YEARS OF DUNSTABLE 1952-1977
A collection of photographs - Bruce Turvey

An era of enormous change in the town, 1952-1977, is commemorated in this superb collection of over 400 photographs — the best from Bruce Turvey's professional collection of over 100,000. Originally published to mark the Queen's Silver Jubilee, her Golden Jubilee seems a fitting moment for its re-issue. Changes include the disappearance of key old landmarks such as the Town Hall, the Red Lion and the California swimming pool, as well as the opening of the prestigious Civic (Queensway) Hall, the circular Catholic Church and the Quadrant Shopping Centre. Here are glimpses of other outstanding occasions, including Whipsnade's 21st Birthday party, the Pageant depicting 750 years of town history, and the granting of the Freedom of the Borough to the Herts and Beds Yeomanry - six years before the town's loss of that status in 1974. Famous visitors abound - four Prime Ministers, along with personalities like Kenneth More, Arthur Askey, David Kossoff, Brenda Lee, George Best, Mary Peters, Hugh Gaitskell and the Duchess of Gloucester. And of course there are hundreds of local people pictured in the photographs of sports teams, coach outings, dinner dances, carnival floats, retirement parties and uniformed organisations. The book opens with a snow scene and closes with a heat wave. In between are the myriad events that comprise the life of a market town during three different decades a generation ago.

STREETS AHEAD
An illustrated guide to the street names of Dunstable - Richard Walden

Over the past 150 years Dunstable has expanded from a small rural market town with limited development beyond the four main streets, to a modern urban town of 35,000 inhabitants and over 300 individual streets. The names of many of those streets have been carefully chosen for some specific reason. Dunstable's modern housing estates in particular have been spared the all too common anonymity of poets, painters, authors and birds found in most other towns. In Dunstable, developers and the local Council have taken great care to select names that record elements of the town's unique historical past and some of the characters and events that helped to shape the local community. Streets Ahead is extensively illustrated with hundreds of photographs and copies of original documents, many of which have never been published before. The content of this work also makes it a fascinating record of the town's recent history.

STICKS & STONES
The life and times of a journeyman printer
Hertford, Dunstable, Cheltenham & Wolverton
Harry Edwards

Sticks and Stones recounts the story of the author's journey through his life in the printing industry, from printer's devil until retirement. Leaving school at the age of fourteen, Harry's transition from schoolboy to apprentice was abrupt. The printing world, with its own language, customs and tradition, was strange at first but most of the journeymen were kind and helpful to a young lad, covering up for many a mistake in the first formative years. The journey begins in Hertfordshire, then takes him on to Bedfordshire, Gloucestershire, London and finally to Buckinghamshire. It follows the author's progress as he seeks not only promotion but also the opportunity to become involved in the latest technology, be it cold type composition, photocomposition, or computer aided typesetting. He touches briefly on his private life when it is appropriate. but the story is primarily about how the changes in the printing industry affected him.

DUNSTABLE IN DETAIL
Nigel C. Benson

Dunstable in Detail is a collection of illustrations and descriptions of 100 features that can all be found within a half mile radius from the centre of Dunstable. The illustrations are accompanied by notes describing points of physical, historical or contemporary interest. As well as the text on the 100 specific features, there are additional notes throughout the book on general topics that are important to this town e.g. local trades, traditions, influential families etc. There are many interesting facets of the town that are not generally recognised by people. All too often travellers think of Dunstable as being just a place to pass through along the A5 or A505 (or pass by on the M1!) and many residents are also unaware of what is around them. The main aim of this book is to help people perceive and appreciate Dunstable's interesting and unique features, and to promote the preservation of that which is of historical and cultural value.

BOURNE AND BRED
A Dunstable boyhood between the wars - Colin Bourne

Colin Bourne talks of the Dunstable he knew from the mid-twenties to the outbreak of war in 1939 - the area where he was brought up, his father's shop, the town characters and the tradesmen, the events, the comings and goings, the Grammar School, the church where he was christened, the Downs and the country close by. A gentle book, laced with his own humour, but with his own opinions too. A reflective and nostalgic look back on a happy boyhood in a South Bedfordshire market town, written by someone who has participated in many of its activities and organisations.

ROYAL HOUGHTON
The story of Houghton Regis Bedfordshire
Pat Lovering

Houghton Regis was a Royal Manor in Saxon times and it appeared in the Domesday Book of 1086. Henry 1st gave land from his Manor of Houghton Regis to make the new town of Dunstable. Read about these and many other fascinating details of the story of Houghton Regis from earliest times to the present day. The book also includes a quick-reference guide to the medieval church of All Saints.

OLD HOUGHTON
including UPPER HOUGHTON now part of DUNSTABLE
Pat Lovering

Old Houghton is a pictorial record of the town, which captures the changing appearance over the last 100 years or so. In this book you can glimpse the past and see the quaint charm of a Bedfordshire village as Houghton Regis was until the late 1950s. It is fascinating to see the Village Pond, the Old Pound Tree and the High Street at the turn of the century. This book shows the importance of recapturing some of Houghton's recent past before it is completely forgotten.

DUNSTABLE DECADE: THE EIGHTIES
A collection of photographs
Pat Lovering

This book celebrates the character and diversity of the town, showing its people, scenes and events during the course of a memorable decade, in nearly three hundred photographs. Dunstable Decade shows great national events echoed in the town - the Falklands conflict, two Royal weddings, and the Armada celebrations. Also shown are the local dramas of flood and fire, Dunstable at play and at work, Dunstable celebrating the arts and honouring its citizens. Pat Lovering has produced an intriguing souvenir for anyone living, working or at leisure in the town during the eighties.

Books Published by THE BOOK CASTLE

COUNTRYSIDE CYCLING IN BEDFORDSHIRE, BUCKINGHAMSHIRE AND HERTFORDSHIRE: Mick Payne. Twenty rides on and off-road for all the family.

PUB WALKS FROM COUNTRY STATIONS: Bedfordshire and Hertfordshire: Clive Higgs. Fourteen circular country rambles, each starting and finishing at a railway station and incorporating a pub stop at a mid way point.

PUB WALKS FROM COUNTRY STATIONS: Buckinghamshire and Oxfordshire: Clive Higgs. Circular rambles incorporating pub-stops.

LOCAL WALKS: South Bedfordshire and North Chilterns: Vaughan Basham. Twenty-seven thematic circular walks.

LOCAL WALKS: North and Mid Bedfordshire: Vaughan Basham. Twenty-five thematic circular walks.

FAMILY WALKS: Chilterns South: Nick Moon. Thirty 3 to 5 mile circular walks.

FAMILY WALKS: Chilterns North: Nick Moon. Thirty shorter circular walks.

CHILTERN WALKS: Hertfordshire, Bedfordshire and North Bucks: Nick Moon.

CHILTERN WALKS: Buckinghamshire: Nick Moon.

CHILTERN WALKS: Oxfordshire and West Buckinghamshire: Nick Moon. A trilogy of circular walks, in association with the Chiltern Society. Each volume contains 30 circular walks.

OXFORDSHIRE WALKS: Oxford, the Cotswolds and the Cherwell Valley: Nick Moon.

OXFORDSHIRE WALKS: Oxford, the Downs and the Thames Valley: Nick Moon. Two volumes that complement Chiltern Walks: Oxfordshire, and complete coverage of the county, in association with the Oxford Fieldpaths Society. Thirty circular walks in each.

THE D'ARCY DALTON WAY: Nick Moon. Long-distance footpath across the Oxfordshire Cotswolds and Thames Valley, with various circular walk suggestions.

THE CHILTERN WAY: Nick Moon. A guide to the new 133 mile circular Long-Distance Path through Bedfordshire, Buckinghamshire,Hertfordshire and Oxfordshire, as planned by the Chiltern Society.

CHANGES IN OUR LANDSCAPE: Aspects of Bedfordshire, Buckinghamshire and the Chilterns 1947-1992: Eric Meadows. Over 350 photographs from the author's collection spanning nearly 50 years.

JOURNEYS INTO BEDFORDSHIRE: Anthony Mackay. Foreword by The Marquess of Tavistock, Woburn Abbey. A lavish book of over 150 evocative ink drawings.

COCKNEY KID & COUNTRYMEN: Ted Enever. The Second World War remembered by the children of Woburn Sands and Aspley Guise. A six year old boy is evacuated from London's East End to start life in a Buckinghamshire village.

BUCKINGHAM AT WAR: Pip Brimson. Stories of courage, humour and pathos as Buckingham people adapt to war.

WINGS OVER WING: The Story of a World War II Bomber Training Unit: Mike Warth. The activities of RAF Wing in Buckinghamshire.

JOURNEYS INTO BUCKINGHAMSHIRE: Anthony Mackay. Superb line drawings plus background text: large format landscape gift book.

BUCKINGHAMSHIRE MURDERS: Len Woodley. Nearly two centuries of nasty crimes.

WINGRAVE: A Rothschild Village in the Vale: Margaret and Ken Morley. Thoroughly researched and copiously illustrated survey of the last 200 years in this lovely village between Aylesbury and Leighton Buzzard.

HISTORIC FIGURES IN THE BUCKINGHAMSHIRE LANDSCAPE: John Houghton. Major personalities and events that have shaped the county's past, including Bletchley Park.

TWICE UPON A TIME: John Houghton.
North Bucks short stories loosely based on fact.

SANCTITY AND SCANDAL IN BEDS AND BUCKS: John Houghton. A miscellany of unholy people and events.

MANORS and MAYHEM, PAUPERS and PARSONS: Tales from Four Shires: Beds., Bucks., Herts. and Northants: John Houghton.
Little known historical snippets and stories.

THE LAST PATROL: Policemen killed on duty while serving the Thames Valley: Len Woodley.

FOLK: Characters and Events in the History of Bedfordshire and Northamptonshire: Vivienne Evans. Anthology of people of yesteryear -arranged alphabetically by village or town.

JOHN BUNYAN: His Life and Times: Vivienne Evans.
Highly praised and readable account.

THE RAILWAY AGE IN BEDFORDSHIRE: Fred Cockman. Classic, illustrated account of early railway history.

A LASTING IMPRESSION: Michael Dundrow. A boyhood evacuee recalls his years in the Chiltern village of Totternhoe near Dunstable.

GLEANINGS REVISITED: Nostalgic Thoughts of a Bedfordshire Farmer's Boy: E.W. O'Dell.
His own sketches and early photographs adorn this lively account of rural Bedfordshire in daysgone by.

BEDFORDSHIRE'S YESTERYEARS: The Rural Scene: Brenda Fraser-Newstead. Vivid first-hand accounts of country life two or three generations ago.

BEDFORDSHIRE'S YESTERYEARS: Craftsmen and Tradespeople: Brenda Fraser-Newstead. Fascinating recollections over several generations practising many vanishing crafts and trades.

BEDFORDSHIRE'S YESTERYEARS: War Times and Civil Matters: Brenda Fraser-Newstead.
Two World Wars, plus transport, law and order, etc.

DUNNO'S ORIGINALS: A facsimile of the rare pre-Victorian history of Dunstable and surrounding villages. New preface and glossary by John Buckledee, Editor of The Dunstable Gazette.

DUNSTABLE DOWN THE AGES: Joan Schneider and Vivienne Evans.
Succinct overview of the town's prehistory and history - suitable for all ages.

HISTORIC INNS OF DUNSTABLE: Vivienne Evans.
Illustrated booklet, especially featuring ten pubs in the town centre.

EXPLORING HISTORY ALL AROUND: Vivienne Evans.
Planned as seven circular car tours, plus background to places of interest en-route in Bedfordshire and parts of Bucks and Herts.

PROUD HERITAGE: A Brief History of Dunstable, 1000-2000AD: Vivienne Evans. Century by century account of the town's rich tradition and key events, many of national significance.

DUNSTABLE WITH THE PRIORY: 1100-1550: Vivienne Evans. Dramatic growth of Henry I's important new town around a major crossroads.

DUNSTABLE IN TRANSITION: 1550-1700: Vivienne Evans. Wealth of original material as the town evolves without the Priory.

DUNSTABLE DECADE: THE EIGHTIES: A Collection of Photographs: Pat Lovering. A souvenir book of nearly 300 pictures of people and events in the 1980's

STREETS AHEAD: An Illustrated Guide to the Origins of Dunstable's Street Names: Richard Walden. Fascinating text and captions to hundreds of photographs, past and present, throughout the town.

DUNSTABLE IN DETAIL: Nigel Benson. A hundred of the town's buildings and features, plus town trail map.

DUNSTAPLE: A Tale of The Watling Highway: A.W. Mooring. Dramatic novelisation of Dunstable's legend of Dunne the Robber - reprinted after a century out of print.

25 YEARS OF DUNSTABLE: Bruce Turvey. Reissue of this photographic treasure-trove of the town up to the Queen's Silver Jubilee, 1952-77.

DUNSTABLE SCHOOL: 1888-1971. F. M. Bancroft. Short history of one of the town's most influential institutions.

BOURNE and BRED: A Dunstable Boyhood Between the Wars: Colin Bourne. An elegantly written, well illustrated book capturing the spirit of the town over fifty years ago.

OLD HOUGHTON: Pat Lovering. Pictorial record capturing the changing appearances of Houghton Regis over the past 100 years.

ROYAL HOUGHTON: Pat Lovering. Illustrated history of Houghton Regis from the earliest of times to the present.

GIRLS IN BLUE: Christine Turner. The activities of the famous Luton Girls Choir properly documented over its 41 year period from 1936 to 1977.

THE STOPSLEY BOOK: James Dyer. Definitive, detailed account of this historic area of Luton. 150 rare photographs.

THE STOPSLEY PICTURE BOOK: James Dyer. New material and photographs make an ideal companion to The Stopsley Book.

PUBS and PINTS: The Story of Luton's Public Houses and Breweries: Stuart Smith. The background to beer in the town, plus hundreds of photographs, old and new.

LUTON AT WAR - VOLUME ONE: As compiled by the Luton News in 1947, a well illustrated thematic account.

LUTON AT WAR - VOLUME TWO: Second part of the book compiled by The Luton News.

THE CHANGING FACE OF LUTON: An Illustrated History: Stephen Bunker, Robin Holgate and Marian Nichols. Luton's development from earliest times to the present busy industrial town. Illustrated in colour and mono.

WHERE THEY BURNT THE TOWN HALL DOWN: Luton, The First World War and the Peace Day Riots, July 1919: Dave Craddock.
Detailed analysis of a notorious incident.

THE MEN WHO WORE STRAW HELMETS: Policing Luton, 1840-1974: Tom Madigan.
Fine chronicled history, many rare photographs; author-served in Luton Police for fifty years.

BETWEEN THE HILLS: The Story of Lilley, a Chiltern Village: Roy Pinnock.
A priceless piece of our heritage - the rural beauty remains but the customs and way of life described here have largely disappeared.

KENILWORTH SUNSET: A Luton Town Supporter's Journal: Tim Kingston.
Frank and funny account of football's ups and downs.

A HATTER GOES MAD!: Kristina Howells. Luton Town footballers, officials and supporters talk to a female fan.

LEGACIES: Tales and Legends of Luton and the North Chilterns: Vic Lea. Mysteries and stories based on fact, including Luton Town Football Club. Many photographs.

THREADS OF TIME: Shela Porter. The life of a remarkable mother and businesswoman, spanning the entire century and based in Hitchin and (mainly) Bedford.

FARM OF MY CHILDHOOD, 1925-1947: Mary Roberts. An almost vanished lifestyle on a remote farm near Flitwick.

STICKS AND STONES: The Life and Times of a Journeyman Printer in Hertford, Dunstable, Cheltenham and Wolverton: Harry Edwards.

CRIME IN HERTFORDSHIRE Volume 1 Law and Disorder: Simon Walker.
Authoritative, detailed survey of the changing legal process over many centuries.

JOURNEYS INTO HERTFORDSHIRE: Anthony Mackay. A foreword by The Marquis of Salisbury, Hatfield House. Introducing nearly 200 superbly detailed line drawings.

LEAFING THROUGH LITERATURE: Writers' Lives in Herts and Beds: David Carroll.
Illustrated short biographies of many famous authors and their connections with these counties.

A PILGRIMAGE IN HERTFORDSHIRE: H.M. Alderman. Classic, between-the-wars tour round the county, embellished with line drawings.

THE VALE OF THE NIGHTINGALE: Molly Andrews. Several generations of a family, lived against a Harpenden backdrop.

SUGAR MICE AND STICKLEBACKS: Childhood Memories of a Hertfordshire Lad: HarryEdwards.Vivid evocation of gentle pre-war in an archetypal village, Hertingfordbury.

SWANS IN MY KITCHEN: Lis Dorer.
Story of a Swan Sanctuary near Hemel Hempstead.

THE HILL OF THE MARTYR: An Architectural History of St.Albans Abbey: Eileen Roberts. Scholarly and readable chronological narrative history of Hertfordshire and Bedfordshire's famous cathedral. Fully illustrated with photographs and plans.

THE TALL HITCHIN INSPECTOR'S CASEBOOK:
A Victorian Crime Novel Based on Fact:
Edgar Newman. Worthies of the time encounter more archetypal villains.

SPECIALLY FOR CHILDREN

VILLA BELOW THE KNOLLS: A Story of Roman Britain: Michael Dundrow. An exciting adventure for young John in Totternhoe and Dunstable two thousand years ago.
THE RAVENS: One Boy Against the Might of Rome: James Dyer. On the Barton Hills and in the south-east of England as the men of the great fort of Ravensburgh (near Hexton) confront the invaders.

TITLES ACQUIRED BY THE BOOK CASTLE

BEDFORDSHIRE WILDLIFE: B.S. Nau, C.R. Boon, J.P. Knowles for the Bedfordshire Natural History Society. Over 200 illustrations, maps, photographs and tables survey the plants and animals of this varied habitat.
BIRDS OF BEDFORDSHIRE: Paul Trodd and David Kramer. Environments, breeding maps and details of 267 species, with dozens of photographs, illustrations and diagrams.
A BEDFORDSHIRE QUIZ BOOK: Eric G. Meadows. Wide ranging quizzes and picture puzzles on the history, people, places and bygones of the county.
CURIOSITIES OF BEDFORDSHIRE: A County Guide to the Unusual:
Pieter and Rita Boogaart.
Quirky, well-illustrated survey of little-known features throughout the county.
THE BIRDS OF HERTFORDSHIRE: Tom Gladwin and Bryan Sage. Essays, maps and records for all 297 species, plus illustrations, photographs and other plates.
BUTTERFLIES OF HERTFORDSHIRE: Brian Sawford. History and ecological guide, with colour photographs and maps for nearly 50 species.
WELWYN RAILWAYS: Tom Gladwin, Peter Neville, Douglas White. A history of the Great Northern line from 1850 to 1986, as epitomised by the five mile stretch between Welwyn Garden City and Woolmer Green. Profusely illustrated in colour and black and white - landscape format.
LIFE AND TIMES OF THE GREAT EASTERN RAILWAY (1839-1922): Harry Paar and Adrian Gray. Personalities, accidents, traffic and tales, plus contemporary photographs and old o.s. maps of this charming railway that transformed East Anglia and Hertfordshire between 1839 and 1922.
THE QUACK: Edgar Newman. Imaginative faction featuring characters in a nineteenth-century painting of a busy Hitchin market scene - especially quack doctor William Mansell.
D-DAY TO ARNHEIM - with Hertfordshire's Gunners: Major Robert Kiln. Vivid, personal accounts of the D-Day preparations and drama, and the subsequent Normandy battles, plus photographs and detailed campaign maps.

THE BOOK CASTLE
12 Church Street, Dunstable,
Bedfordshire LU5 4RU
Tel: (01582) 605670 Fax (01582) 662431
Email: bc@book-castle.co.uk